THE HISTORIC
ST. CROIX VALLEY

THE HISTORIC ST. CROIX VALLEY

A Guided Tour

Deborah Morse-Kahn

Minnesota Historical
Society Press

www.mhspress.org

The Minnesota Historical Society Press is a member of the Association of American University Presses.

Manufactured in U.S.A.

10 9 8 7 6 5 4 3 2 1

∞ The paper used in this publication meets the minimum requirements of the American National Standard for Information Sciences—Permanence for Printed Library Materials, ANSI Z39.48–1984.

Credits
Front cover: © iStockphoto.com/Lawrence Sawyer
Back cover: *Judd Street Looking North 1906,* Carl Arthur Ecklund, MHS collections
Interior: images pages 162 and 198, Wisconsin Historical Society. All others, MHS collections.
Maps: CartoGraphics Inc.
Design: Percolator

International Standard Book Number
ISBN: 978-0-87351-774-4 (paper)
ISBN: 978-0-87351-799-7 (e-book)

Library of Congress Cataloging-in-Publication Data
Morse-Kahn, Deborah, 1952–
    The historic St. Croix valley : a guided tour /
    Deborah Morse-Kahn.
        p. cm.
    Includes bibliographical references and index.
    ISBN 978-0-87351-774-4 (pbk. : alk. paper)
        1. Saint Croix River Valley Region (Wis. and Minn.)—Tours.
        2. Historic sites—Saint Croix River Valley Region
            (Wis. and Minn.)—Guidebooks.
        3. Historic buildings—Saint Croix River Valley Region
            (Wis. and Minn.)—Guidebooks.
        4. Saint Croix River Valley Region (Wis. and Minn.)—
            History, Local.
        I. Title. II. Title: Historic Saint Croix valley.
F612.S2M67 2010
977.6′59—dc22
                                                    2010013527

For James Taylor Dunn (1912–2002)
Historian, Librarian, Advocate, Educator, Author
Protector and Biographer of the St. Croix River

CONTENTS

PREFACE

This book was written as historic structures were being razed and stories of entire cities were being swept away in the path of modern improvements. As always, such documentation and description has come just in time, if not perhaps a moment too late, since it takes real loss for us to rally in the effort to preserve markers of our collective past. And as always, such documentation and description can help the generations that both see their past as a thing of great worth and want to know more.

The St. Croix Valley's history has so many facets. In the midst of spectacular geography and geology, First Nation peoples, European traders, and immigrants who founded villages made use of the river and its natural gifts to survive. Industry and commerce became the driving force of life on the St. Croix from the 1840s forward, leaving for us physical reminders in stone and brick for shelter, for civic endeavor, and for industry. Many of these physical markers have been lost over 150 years, but marvelous examples still stand, at home in a river valley landscape that remains remarkably unchanged since the days of territorial designation.

And finally, the river itself is in parts wild and untamed and in others controlled and corralled. Environmental management of the St. Croix River has been a one-hundred-year undertaking and continues with passion today.

May this book further encourage the preservation of the entire St. Croix Valley, for us, for those who have passed and gone, and for our children and their children.

Overview: The St. Croix Valley

THE HISTORIC
ST. CROIX VALLEY

THE ST. CROIX STORY

The St. Croix River is a peaceful passage between modern cities that joins the great Mississippi and mingles with its waters. It is also, at one point, a placid and beautiful lake, a small sea from side to side, along which for thousands of years people have found shelter, sustenance, and a sustainable way of life. The river has been controlled—dammed, managed, and modified—for modern business needs and less treacherous passage, yet it also remains a wild river, flowing freely, rushing south, and joining hands with its tributaries large and small. A magnificent ecosystem has evolved that, today, we honor, preserve, conserve, and monitor with great care.

For thousands of years, though, the St. Croix—from its natural glacial dam in the northwest of present-day Wisconsin to its confluence with a much larger sibling, the Mississippi River—was a source of food, a source of transport, and a source of seasonal sustenance in furs, bark, rushes, blueberries, and drinking water for Native Americans.

Eventually, the Native Americans in this area made contact with European explorers, then trappers and traders, and then entire trading companies. The lands of the new territories were explored, described, and surveyed. Fur traders, speaking English, French, and Algonquian languages, who had partnered for commerce stayed for a lifetime, often marrying women from their Native American trading villages.

The American Fur Company promoted the establishment of trading posts; the federal government built forts to keep order in the raw new lands. The French had made their own mark on the land and on the water

Dalles of the St. Croix, Elijah Evan Edwards, 1880

and on its peoples, and the voyageurs, *les coureurs de bois* ("carriers of the woods"), gave this great river its name.

Treaties were written with tribal nations, offering federal support and guaranteed trade, in exchange for lands burgeoning with white pine and minerals. The Treaty of 1837 ceded the pineries to the American government. Again and again, the Ojibwe, Dakota, Ho-Chunk, Fox, Sac, and Mesqwaki nations were herded into ever tighter blocks of land and were forced into dependence on the European benefactors through annuities and, increasingly, alcohol.

Lands belonging to these tribes were taken away, sometimes honorably, frequently dishonorably, and using these lands and what grew there—timber—the Wisconsin and Minnesota territories helped to build an empire, establish new states in the Union, and make a great many people extraordinarily wealthy. The valley and its industry provided a haven for immigrants for whom life at home—the impoverished farmlands of Sweden, the religious oppression of France, the barren potato fields of Ireland—was no longer sustainable.

Lumber was in such plenty that men moved inland from the river and took as much as they could, long before the federal government had given permission to cut the old-growth forests of white pine, oak, maple, and

Ojibwe on the St. Croix, c1885

walnut. By the 1850s, lumbering was the occupation of area entrepreneurs, who founded logging companies and built mills to saw what the company employees had sent downriver. The camps in the pineries in winter were brutal and basic, but it was honest labor, gave a man good, hard work, and also provided that uniquely American event—the mingling of many ethnicities and races for a common cause. In their time the Swedes and the Italians worked among the Ojibwe and the English and the Irish and the Germans. And all who could farm did so, and those who could not planted vegetable gardens.

Men grew rich and built great houses on high hilltops above prospering towns. The federal government commissioned a road to be built atop old Ojibwe and Dakota trails, enabling the movement of hundreds of thousands of people up and down the St. Croix River, from its confluence with the Brule all the way south to its meeting with the Mississippi. Many towns flourished beyond expectation, and their wealth of architecture and planning remains today. Many towns waxed and waned, according to the dictates of the national lumber industry. Some were dreamed of but never came into being. Great towns and cities existed only as sketches

Logjam at Taylors Falls, 1844

on maps, platted for a hundred blocks of prosperous citizens and magnificent civic structures and found a hundred years later in old desk drawers in empty houses in abandoned towns.

The Civil War united the St. Croix Valley population in a way no other crisis could have. Men of every ethnicity formed volunteer regiments, left their homes, their farms, their sawmills, and their families, and went to war. In their absence entire communities banded together for the aid and support of the families left behind and, later, for the care of the grievously wounded when they came home or for payment of the burial of a pine casket when it was unloaded from a steamboat or train car. In many instances, smaller towns lost most of their younger men to the war. The cemeteries of the St. Croix Valley are filled with pioneer graveyards sheltering the Civil War dead, among whom are many immigrants who had been in the United States less than six months.

The St. Croix Valley's lumber era peaked in 1880 and began to decline rapidly in 1906 with the installation of the St. Croix Hydroelectric Power Dam. Visible remnants of the logging industry would remain for years. The Nevers Dam upstream at Wolf Creek, the largest wooden

Civil War survivors at Veterans Day observance, Marine on St. Croix, c1920

dam in its time—installed to control the flow of water and thus the flow of logs—was left in place but is no longer used for its original mission. New times had come with the railroad and then the automobile. River traffic faded, and the first true tourists came east from the large cities inland to admire the beauty of the St. Croix Valley and to stay to fish and relax and, if sufficient desire and money coincided, build a summer home.

By the end of World War I, several of the Lake St. Croix villages were beginning to tear down the last remnants of the old saw and flouring mills and sell the land for cabins and resorts. A silver lining showed through the hard times of the Depression when the Civilian Conservation Corps (CCC) set up camps in the region and began work on the beautification of river-area parks and overlooks or built handsome and architecturally unique structures in state parks on both sides of the river. Roads were improved, bridges rebuilt, parks refurbished, and tourism promoted in a way never seen before in the region.

After World War II, the towns on the St. Croix began to see a steady increase in house building and population, an ever-growing number of the new townsfolk driving back into the Twin Cities for employment.

By the mid-1960s, local, regional, and national environmental and historical coalitions began to look at the fast development of the St. Croix Valley—particularly Lake St. Croix—with alarm and with care and considerable skill began to press their concerns through legislative representatives and media resources.

Picnicking at Taylors Falls, c1900

Concern over both the river and its ecosystem and the historic remnants of other eras came to the fore in the 1970s. There were good years and rough years. The upper St. Croix won federal designation as a National Scenic Riverway in 1968; the lower St. Croix was added in 1972. The state historical societies of Minnesota and Wisconsin finished their first detailed reviews of historic properties and sites in preparation for protection of buildings and districts tied to the states' stories. A bridge project has been indefinitely stalled, but not without great losses, including an entire town's historic core. And there have been victories small and large. National Register Districts have been established for intact villages, and tiny populations of riparian flora and fauna found nowhere else in the world have been preserved.

Today, it is possible to know a lot about the communities that line this special river. We want that knowledge not only because the stories of Native Americans and European settlers who arrived here are part of our state identification but because there are critical lessons to be learned, and great joy to be had, in the knowledge that, come what may, people who have passed are just like us. They lived as best they could and made decisions alone or together. We are the stewards of the results of those decisions.

ST. CROIX VALLEY TRAVEL RESOURCES

St. Croix National Scenic Riverway
401 Hamilton Street
PO Box 708 (mailing address)
St. Croix Falls, WI 54024
715-483-3284
www.nps.gov/sacn

Minnesota St. Croix Scenic Byway
25156 St. Croix Trail North
Shafer, MN 55074
info@stcroixscenicbyway.org
www.stcroixscenicbyway.org

Minnesota Historical Society
345 Kellogg Boulevard West
St. Paul, MN 55102
651-259-3000
www.mnhs.org

Minnesota Historical Society National Register of Historic Places Database
http://nrhp.mnhs.org/nrsearch.cfm

Wisconsin Historical Society Library and Archives
816 State Street
Madison, WI 53706-1417
608-264-6535
www.wisconsinhistory.org

Wisconsin National Register of Historic Places
www.wisconsinhistory.org/hp/register

St. Croix River Association
PO Box 1032
Hudson, WI 54016
715-483-2292
www.stcroixriverassociation.org

St. Croix Scenic Coalition
PO Box 508
St. Croix Falls, WI 54024
www.stcroixsceniccoalition.org

St. Croix Collection
Stillwater Public Library
224 North 3rd Street
Stillwater, MN 55082
651-275-4338
splinfo@ci.stillwater.mn.us
www.stillwaterlibrary.org

COUNTY HISTORICAL SOCIETIES

Dakota County Historical Society
130 3rd Avenue North
South St. Paul, MN 55075-2002
651-552-7548
www.dakotahistory.org

Washington County Historical Society
602 Main Street North
Stillwater, MN 55082-4010
651-439-5956
information@wchsmn.org
www.wchsmn.org

South Washington Heritage Society
www.usfamily.net/web/albyrobinson

Chisago County History Center
13100 3rd Avenue North
PO Box 146 (mailing address)
Lindström, MN 55045-0146
651-257-5310
www.chisagocountyhistory.org

Wisconsin Historical Society Area Research Center
Burnett, Pierce, Polk, and St. Croix Counties
University of Wisconsin–River Falls
410 South 3rd Street

River Falls, WI 54022
715-425-3567
archives@uwrf.edu
www.uwrf.edu/library/arc

Pierce County Historical Society
130 North Chestnut Street
Ellsworth, WI 54011
715-273-6611
info@piercecountyhistorical.org
www.piercecountyhistorical.org

St. Croix County Historical Society
The Octagon House Museum
1004 3rd Street
Hudson, WI 54016
715-386-2654
octagonhousemuseum@juno.com
www.pressenter.com/~octagon

Polk County Information Center
710 Highway 35
St. Croix Falls, WI 54024
800-222-7655
www.polkcountytourism.com

Polk County Historical Society
120 Main Street
Balsam Lake, WI 54810-0311
715-485-9269
darose@centurytel.net
www.co.polk.wi.us/history

Pine County Historical Society
64385 Hammond Road
Finlayson, MN 55735
320-245-2574

Pine County History Museum
Askov Depot
Main Street

Askov, MN 55704
320-838-3665

LODGING AND RECREATION

St. Croix Valley Regional Tourism Alliance
PO Box 387
Osceola, WI 54020
651-439-4001
info@saintcroixriver.com
www.saintcroixriver.com

Explore Minnesota Tourism
888-868-7476
explore@state.mn.us
www.exploreminnesota.com

Travel Wisconsin
Wisconsin Department of Tourism
201 West Washington Avenue
PO Box 8690 (mailing address)
Madison, WI 53708-8690
608-266-2161
800-432-8747
www.travelwisconsin.com

Minnesota Bed and Breakfast Association
620 Ramsey Street
Hastings, MN 55033
651-438-7499
info@minnesotabedandbreakfasts.org
www.minnesotabedandbreakfasts.org

Wisconsin Bed and Breakfast Association
108 South Cleveland Street
Merrill, WI 54452
715-539-9222
info@wbba.org
www.wbba.org

Posing on tree overhanging St. Croix River, 1917

MINNESOTA

HASTINGS AND NININGER

HASTINGS: GRAIN AS DESTINY

The architecturally rich city of Hastings sits, like its sister city Prescott, Wisconsin, at the point where the lower St. Croix flows into the Mississippi and forms Lake St. Croix. Though Prescott is considered the older settlement, Hastings had outstripped its rival by the mid-nineteenth century.

The siting of the settlement of Hastings, known as early as 1819 as Oliver's Grove, was an ideal location for a military encampment sent up the river from Fort Snelling. Blessed with a natural deep harbor for shipping and the fast-flowing Vermillion River (called by the Dakota *Wa-Śe-Śa Wa-Kpá*, or the Red Paint River), whose falls dropped dramatically over the bluffs to the Mississippi below, Oliver's Grove naturally attracted more settlers and, eventually, a trading post established in 1833 by Joseph R. Brown. Brown was working then as an independent trader with Henry Hastings Sibley's American Fur Company. He would go on to plat the city of Dakotah up the river in the 1840s (a town later renamed Stillwater) and eventually play significant roles in the state's political history. Later, in 1850, Alexis Bailly had his son, Henry, establish a trading post at the tiny village so that he could claim the land when it opened for settlement.

With the Treaty of Mendota in 1851, which relocated the Dakota tribes to reservations, extraordinary land speculation and settlement began in the lower St. Croix Valley. By 1857, Oliver's Grove had been incorporated as a city and given the name Hastings (one of several choices offered by Henry Hastings Sibley, who was to become Minnesota's first governor within the year).

With the added prestige of Sibley's partners—Alexander Faribault, Alexis Bailly, and Bailly's son, Henry—also came its designation as the new seat of government for Dakota County. Faribault departed soon after the city's founding, selling his quarter share to William G. LeDuc and moving west where he would successfully develop a new town to which he gave his own name. The Baillys and Sibley also moved on, but LeDuc settled permanently in Hastings.

Hastings's first settlers were primarily Germans, Scandinavians, and immigrants from the United Kingdom, drawn by the opportunity for construction work in the rapidly growing town, the creation of new lumber and grain mills, the rich soil of the Vermillion River plains, and, especially for the Germans, an abundance of springs and spring-fed lakes for beer brewing. Other new settlers were drawn to the region from East Coast states such as New York, looking for new opportunities and

Vermillion River falls below Hastings, c1865

cheaper land. They arrived primarily by steamboats that also carried supplies, grain, lumber, and tourists. From 1857 to 1865, Hastings grew by 2,500 citizens.

Grain milling became serious business in 1853 when Harrison H. Graham developed a technique of grinding that produced what came to be known as "graham flour" (not to be confused with the Rev. Sylvester Graham's millings, first marketed in 1829, which are still used in graham crackers). Graham built a modest millhouse and dam on the upper falls of the Vermillion River on the south end of the town.

In 1857, Hastings's second grain mill was built by Thomas Foster and Alexander Ramsey—in the years between his service as the first territorial governor and election as Minnesota's second governor—at the lower falls of the Vermillion River. With a fifty-foot-wide stream dropping nineteen feet below the milldam, the two-and-a-half-story stone mill came to be known as the Ramsey Mill and a major producer of high-quality flour, reaching a 125-barrel-a-day capacity. This finely milled wheat was successfully marketed under romantic names such as Belle of Hastings Flour and Pearl of Hastings Flour.

Stephen Gardner bought Harrison Graham's mill in 1863 and eventually built a much larger grain mill and elevator incorporating many new and innovative milling technologies, including a cooperage producing specially designed flour barrels. At its height, the Gardner mill was producing over one thousand barrels a day. The

Hastings before the Civil War, c1855

Gardner mill was soon a principal factor in establishing Hastings's regional reputation as a grain and malting power.

By 1868, the first railroads into Hastings began to compete fiercely with riverboat traffic as a means of moving goods and people. The Hastings and Dakota Railroad built a line between the town of Lakeville and the new depot and roundhouse in Hastings, later absorbed as part of the much larger Chicago, Milwaukee and St. Paul Railroad. Faster, more comfortable, and dependable as year-round transportation, the railroads soon replaced passenger and shipping boats and contributed steadily to Hastings's growth. The CM&StP built a magnificent new swing bridge over the Mississippi in 1871, one of the first iron railroad bridges in the state. By the 1870s, Hastings's levee was a solid and broad expanse of grain elevators, sawmills, foundries, warehouses, and loading docks; the county had constructed a vast and spectacular courthouse near the city center; and Hastings's population had jumped to 3,400.

Another venture in railroading came in 1880 with the building of the Stillwater and Hastings branch line, its singular purpose being to transport lumber, grain, and farm produce between the two growing cities. Within two years the Milwaukee Road had bought out the line to its great profit.

The year 1895 saw the building of a new bridge, this one designed in a spiral solely to slow down horse-drawn traffic over the river and deliver the carts, buggies, and sledges at a modest pace into Hastings's bustling business district. The exotic and very lovely wooden bridge was an immediate tourist draw, and travelers by steamboat and rail always made a stop to admire the unique bridge and buy a postcard of it as a memento.

By the turn of the century, Hastings's wealth was clearly evident. The city could boast block after block of fine residential structures, large and handsome churches, a magnificent county courthouse, lovely public parks,

Spiral bridge, Hastings, c1920

an opera house, a beautiful three-story stone and brick high school (with many roof gables and an enormous cupola), several large breweries, and numerous hotels and taverns to serve pocketbooks of all sizes.

Hastings was also now the site of a unique and carefully designed hospital, the Second State Asylum for the Insane. Perched high on a knoll above the river, far from the city center, the beautiful brick Tudor Revival structures were built in the cottage plan to permit a more homelike atmosphere for the patients. Additional administrative and maintenance buildings would be added over time, all reflecting the original architectural intention. The hospital's name was changed several times over the years, first to the Hastings State Asylum (1919) and then to the Hastings State Hospital (1937). The massive campus was rededicated as a state veterans' home in 1978.

Change came rapidly to Hastings at the end of the century. The Ramsey mill was lost to a fire in 1894, marking the end of thirty-seven years of steady production. The Graham-Gardner mill was bought out in 1897 by Seymour Carter, who continued to enlarge the milling campus and expand operations. Carter sold his mill after fifteen years of production to partners out of

Philadelphia who had been producing flour under the King Midas brand. Fred and George Shane and W. J. Wilson had the old Graham-Gardner-Carter mill renamed the King Midas Mill, producing not only fine white flour but also hard durum wheat flour used primarily in the making of pastas such as spaghetti and flat egg noodles. Demand for millhands, carters, rail workers, carpenters, dockhands, and other skilled labor brought Hastings's population to a new high of 4,500.

The years after World War I saw the withdrawal of federal price supports for many of the country's agricultural products and, in 1924, the King Midas mill came under the ownership of the Minneapolis flour milling titan the Peavey Company, which kept the King Midas name for its immediate market recognition and reputation for high quality. The post–World War I years brought further development to Hastings when the Army Corps of Engineers undertook construction of the Mississippi River's Lock and Dam No. 2, which was completed in 1930.

The county and state carried out massive road and highway improvement projects starting in the 1950s, including replacing the deteriorating wooden spiral bridge with a new straight-line steel structure that today carries

Second Street looking east, Hastings, c1905

an average of 32,000 vehicles across the Mississippi on Highway 61 daily and has for many years been famous (or infamous) for being the busiest two-lane highway bridge in the state of Minnesota (construction of a much larger bridge is expected to begin in 2010).

Frank Lloyd Wright would not live to see the completion of the last of his more than eight hundred architectural masterpieces, the Dr. Herman Fasbender Clinic, completed two months after his death in 1959.

The Milwaukee Road, which bought the little Stillwater and Hastings line in 1880, continued to operate it for nearly one hundred years, with its end coming in 1979.

The Dakota County Courthouse saw the removal of all county personnel and offices to a new modern facility in 1989. The City of Hastings purchased the historic structure and rededicated the beautiful building as the new city hall in 1993, serving a community that had reached a population of nearly 20,000.

Not everything of historic value has survived in Hastings. Nearly all railroad structures have been razed, leaving a sadly depleted tract of land. Virtually the entirety of the foundries, warehouses, mills, and elevators that once lined the Hastings levee is also gone, replaced with a vast and open green space. Historic interpretive panels depicting what once existed and has now been lost have been placed along the railings of a concrete pier built for the new replica steamboats that carry visitors up and down Lake St. Croix.

But several of the city's wonderful historic residential neighborhoods are beautifully intact due to a community well aware of its inheritance and determined to see individual buildings and entire districts receive care and local or national historic designation. And a busy and very knowledgeable chamber of commerce and tourism office is found in Hastings's historic business district, promoting what has become one of Hastings's most important commodities—tourism.

NININGER: THE LOST CITY

The town was founded and named by John Nininger, brother-in-law of territorial and state governor Alexander Ramsey. Nininger, strongly influenced by Philadelphia politician and philosopher Ignatius Donnelly's vision of a communal utopian village, platted an ambitious townsite in 1857 three miles north of the town of Hastings with hopes that Nininger would become Minnesota's state capitol.

Donnelly printed and distributed posters and leaflets promoting Nininger as the "Chicago of the North" to immigrants and settlers in other regions, states, and even countries (Scotland). Within one year the townsite could boast nearly one hundred houses and a population just under one thousand, served by numerous stores, several churches, a dance hall, a school, a Good Templars hall that doubled as a gathering site for a summer lyceum and lectures, a flour mill, and several lumber mills. The mills provided materials for the building of an exceptional number of opulent and very handsome houses on large parklands, including Donnelly's own residence.

The financial panic of 1857 brought a swift end to Nininger, and within the first twelve months after the town's establishment, the first house of many was being rafted downriver to be resettled in Hastings by Ignatius Eckert. The financial panic also sounded the death knell for the land-grant program for railroads. Donnelly had counted on the building of a line to be named the Nininger, St. Peter, and Western Railroad to support the new town's economic stability and growth. Donnelly was financially ruined.

Houses—and their occupants—continued to disappear from Nininger, and within five years most of the townsite had been vacated. The post office continued in service until 1889. Soon little was left except some farms, a stretch of the government road built in the 1830s, and the Templars hall.

But Donnelly stayed on, refusing to leave the grand house he had built and the vast library it contained, where he spent much of his time writing and ruminating. He entered politics and was elected lieutenant governor of Minnesota from 1860 to 1863 and followed up with service as Minnesota's Republican congressman through 1868 and as state senator from 1874 to 1878. Donnelly fought for legislative support for the Freedmen's Bureau that had been established for freed slaves in the first years of Reconstruction following the Civil War. He was also an early supporter of woman's suffrage and worked tirelessly for the cause.

When Donnelly secured a seat in the state legislature, he heeded the national farm alliance movement's call and became an organizer of Minnesota's chapter. After working for the People's Party in the 1890s, Donnelly ran for governor of Minnesota but lost the election.

When his wife, Katherine, died in 1894, Donnelly at last left his mansion sitting among the empty fields of the ghost town of Nininger and moved into Minneapolis. He died there in 1901, leaving his books and papers to the Minnesota Historical Society.

The Nininger School became the township hall in 1951 and underwent major restoration in the late 1970s.

Ignatius Donnelly and family at Nininger, c1893

It was successfully placed on the National Register in 1980. In 2005, Nininger Township's citizens voted to build a new facility and the historic town hall was sold for one dollar to the Little Log House Pioneer Village south of Hastings.

Pilgrims to the failed townsite were permitted a tour of Donnelly's intact house well into the late 1930s. Tenants of the Donnelly house were required to keep the house interior well maintained, with all its original furniture and a great many of Donnelly's personal belongings. A guest book that Donnelly had always kept in the foyer of his grand home for his many visitors remained in place, and guests continued to enter their names and the dates of their visits.

Efforts to save the house failed, and it was razed in 1949. Today, several historic markers at the intersection of 125th Street East and Ivanhoe Avenue, the site of the new town hall, and the stretch of road marked out as a government road offer the story of both the Donnelly house and Good Templars hall. Beautiful farms surround the old townsite, a reminder of the dreams once held by Ignatius Donnelly of the possibilities of communal farms, worked by all and providing for all.

ⓘ LOCAL RESOURCES

Hastings Area Chamber of Commerce and Tourism Bureau
111 East 3rd Street
Hastings, MN 55033
651-437-6775
888-612-6122
info@hastingsmn.org
www.hastingsmn.org
Visitors may pick up scenic bike trail and self-guided historic walking tour brochures.

City of Hastings Pioneer Room
Hastings City Hall
101 East 4th Street
Hastings, MN 55033

continues

Curator: 651-480-2367
csmith@ci.hastings.mn.us
Open Monday and Wednesday from 8:00 a.m. to 4:30 p.m.
and Thursday from 8:00 a.m. to noon.

LeDuc Historic Estate
1629 Vermillion Street
Hastings, MN 55033
651-437-7055
leduc@co.dakota.mn.us
www.dakotahistory.org
Open late May thru late October.

Little Log House Pioneer Village and Antique Power Show
21889 Michael Avenue (6 miles south of downtown Hastings)
Hastings, MN 55033
651-437-2693
www.littleloghouseshow.com

LODGING OPTIONS

Classic Rosewood Inn Bed and Breakfast
620 Ramsey Street
Hastings, MN 55033
651-437-3297 or 888-846-7966
info@thorwoodinn.com
www.classicrosewood.com

The Arbor Bed and Breakfast Inn
434 North Court Street
Prescott, WI 54021
715-262-2222 or 888-262-1090
relax@thearborinn.com
www.thearborinn.com

Historic Afton House Inn and Afton-Hudson Cruise Lines
3291 St. Croix Trail South
Afton, MN 55001
651-436-8883 or 877-436-8883
info@aftonhouseinn.com
www.aftonhouseinn.com

HASTINGS AND NININGER TOUR

See map on p. 27.

The city of Hastings has sixty-three National Register buildings, of which thirty-three are commercial buildings, twenty-eight are residential buildings, and two are churches. Many of these buildings are contained within two National Register Districts.

"NR" indicates National Register properties.

1. RAMSEY MILL RUINS (1857, NR) AND OLD MILL PARK (1925, NR)

Best approached from north park entrance on East 18th Street; turn east off of Vermillion Street when you see the ConAgra buildings. The ruins of the mill are still to be seen in the Old Mill Park, the broken pillars of worked stone evoking a sense of haunting loss. Excellent interpretive signage. Paved path is mostly accessible, except for the final few steps down to a railed-off platform above mill ruins. Park along street. No facilities or picnic sites. Paved pathway leads across park to Graham-Gardner Mill site.

2. MINNESOTA VETERANS' HOME (FORMERLY SECOND STATE ASYLUM FOR THE INSANE, 1900)
Immediately east of Old Mill Park on East 18th Street

3. GRAHAM-GARDNER MILL (1853, EXPANDED 1863) AND VERMILLION FALLS PARK

Outstanding view of upper falls and of rear of historic mill buildings, including mechanical works but no interpretive signage. Parking lot, no facilities, but several picnic shelters. Accessibility possible but challenging due to steep slopes. Paved pathway leads across park to Old Mill Ruins site.

4. LEDUC HISTORIC ESTATE (1866, NR)
1629 Vermillion Street

Built by William and Mary LeDuc, an early investor in the land that came to be platted as Hastings. Mary LeDuc selected the Victorian Gothic design from the book *Cottage Residences,* published in 1842 by Andrew Jackson Downing, whose designs were modeled on the "cottage" homes of the wealthy of New York's Hudson River Valley. Now owned by the City of Hastings and managed by the Dakota County Historical Society as a fully restored historic site open to the public for tours and events. Civil War encampment reenactment on the estate every first full weekend in September.

LeDuc family on porch, Hastings, c1910

5. VERMILLION RIVER: UPPER LEVEE LANDING PARK

6. HASTINGS METHODIST EPISCOPAL CHURCH (1862, NR)
8th Street and Vermillion Street

7. HOWES-GRAUS HOUSE (1868, NR)
718 Vermillion Street

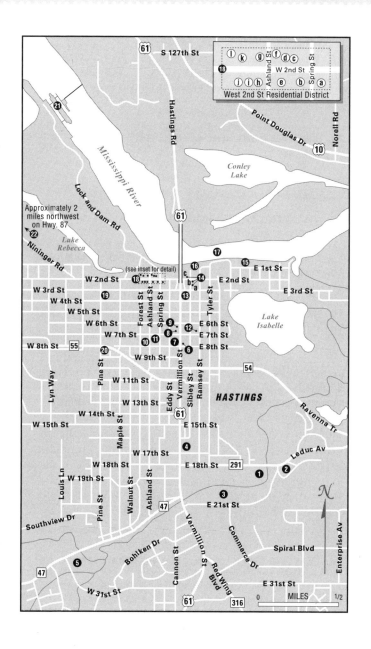

West 2nd St Residential District

(l) (k) (g) Ashland St (f)(d)(c) Spring St
(18)   W 2nd St
(j)(i)(h) Ashland St (e)   (b) (a)

(61) S 127th St

Point Douglas Dr

Norell Rd

(10)

Conley Lake

Hastings Rd

(21)

Mississippi River

(61)

Lock and Dam Rd

Approximately 2
miles northwest
on Hwy. 87

(22)

Lake Rebecca

Nininger Rd

(17)

(16)   E 1st St

(15)

(see inset for detail)   c
W 2nd St   b   E 2nd St
(18)   (14)
W 3rd St   a   E 3rd St
(19)   (13)

W 4th St   Tyler St

W 5th St   Lake
Isabelle
W 6th St   Forest St Ashland St Spring St (9)   E 6th St
(10)(11) (8) E 7th St
W 7th St   (7)
(12)
W 8th St   55   (6)   E 8th St
(20)
W 9th St
54

Pine St

W 11th St

Lyn Way   *HASTINGS*

W 13th St   Eddy St Vermillion St Sibley St Ramsey St   Ravenna Tr

W 14th St

Maple St

W 15th St
E 15th St
(61)

W 17th St   (4)

Leduc Av

W 18th St   E 18th St   291
Louis Ln
W 19th St   (1) (2)

Pine St   Walnut St Ashland St   (3)
47   E 21st St

Southview Dr

N

Bohlken Dr

Cannon St

Vermillion St Red Wing Blvd

Commerce Dr

Spiral Blvd

Enterprise Av

(5)
47
E 31st St

W 31st St
(61)   316   0   MILES   1/2

8. VAN DYKE-LIBBEY HOUSE (1868, NR)
612 Vermillion Street

9. FIRST UNITED PRESBYTERIAN CHURCH (C. 1881)
602 Vermillion Street

10. ECKERT-WRIGHT HOUSE (1850, NR)
724 Ashland Avenue

The Nininger Townsite Houses (NR)

11. MACDONALD-TODD HOUSE (1857, NR)
309 West 7th Street

12. RUDOLPH LATTO HOUSE/LATTO HOSPITAL (C. 1880, NR)
620 Ramsey Street

13. HISTORIC DAKOTA COUNTY COURTHOUSE (1871, NR)
101 East 4th Street

The courthouse was under construction by 1868 and completed three years later at the cost of $95,000. The designer, A. M. Radcliffe, enjoyed using a variety of European architectural flourishes, including German styling in its square shape and towers, French Renaissance tower domes, Italian Florentine window arches in stone, and Greek Corinthian columns at the main public entrance. The dome and rotunda at the center of the building were added during an extensive remodeling in 1912 (architect P. Donivan), and several additions to the courthouse were made in later decades. Hastings's city hall took up quarters in the historic courthouse in 1993.

14. EAST 2ND STREET COMMERCIAL HISTORIC DISTRICT (NR)

This National Register historic district contains thirty-five buildings that made up the heart of Hastings's nineteenth-century river town commercial life.

14a. OLD CITY HALL (1884, NR)
215 Sibley Street

Commercial Italianate style designed by architects Powers and Metzker.

14b. OLD POST OFFICE (1868)
200 East 2nd Street

Commercial Italianate style.

14c. ADSIT HOSPITAL (1912)
117 to 119 East 2nd Street

Commercial Queen Anne style.

15. HASTINGS FOUNDRY/STAR IRON WORKS (1859, NR)
707 East 1st Street

One of the earliest industrial buildings remaining in Minnesota.

16. LEVEE PARK
East 1st Street, west of Ramsey Street

17. CHICAGO, MILWAUKEE AND ST. PAUL RAILROAD HIGH BRIDGE (1871)

18. HASTINGS WEST 2ND STREET RESIDENTIAL DISTRICT (NR)

There are thirteen architecturally significant homes in this National Register district, built between 1857 and 1890, many reflecting architectural styles in vogue in the second half of the nineteenth century.

18a. STRAUSS HOUSE (1875)
207 West 2nd Street

18b. CLAFLIN-NORRISH HOUSE (C. 1858)
302 West 2nd Street

One of only some one hundred octagon structures built in Minnesota before 1900.

18c. O'SHAUGHNESSY HOUSE (1885)
312 West 2nd Street

18d. LAMMO HOUSE (1880)
314 West 2nd Street

18e. THORNE/LOWELL HOUSE (1861)
319 West 2nd Street

18f. MATSCH HOUSE (1865)
322 West 2nd Street

18g. ELLINGBOE RESIDENCE (1885)
400 West 2nd Street

18h. RADAUGH HOUSE (1890)
401 West 2nd Street

18i. MAIRS HOUSE (1857)
409 West 2nd Street

18j. PRINGLE HOUSE (1870)
413 West 2nd Street

18k. OLSON HOUSE (1851)
414 to 416 West 2nd Street

18l. PRINGLE/CLAGETT HOUSE (1858)
418 West 2nd Street

19. THOMPSON-FASBENDER HOUSE (1880, NR)
649 West 3rd Street

20. FASBENDER CLINIC (1959, NR)
801 Pine Street

21. MISSISSIPPI RIVER LOCK AND DAM NO. 2 (1930)

Take Lock and Dam Boulevard north from East 2nd Street

Free observatory during open-water seasons.

NININGER

2½ miles northwest of Hastings on County Road 87

22. NININGER TOWNSHIP HALL (1857, NR) AND HISTORIC MARKERS

Founded and named by John Nininger, brother-in-law of territorial and state governor Alexander Ramsey. The township hall, now modernized for accessibility, is of simple white clapboard; its original construction outlines can still be seen despite modifications. The two historic markers describing the Ignatius Donnelly home and the Good Templars hall are on your right at Ivanhoe Avenue, which itself is an extension of the original Point Douglas–Superior territorial road.

POINT DOUGLAS AND DENMARK TOWNSHIP

POINT DOUGLAS: GHOSTS OF THE PAST

It's hard to imagine a large town once existed on the point of land where Washington County Road 21, known as the St. Croix Trail, leaves Highway 10 and, making a deep sweep to the south, rights itself to head due north. Just at the broad curve of the road, down toward the shore, was the Point Douglas commercial and milling district. Up the hill were the residential district, the school, and the churches. The last of the buildings were moved some years ago to private properties in Denmark Township.

The long point of land on the western side of the lower St. Croix River forms a peninsula where the Mississippi River meets the St. Croix and was home to native peoples for centuries. The presence of Dakota villages at the confluence of the two rivers (in Dakota, *O-Ki-Źu Wa-Kpá,* or Where River Water Gathers into a Lake) was recorded by many European traders and explorers, including Joseph N. Nicollet, who also called it "the place where the waters gather and the rivers meet."

O-Ki-Źu Wa-Kpá became the site of a vicious confrontation in 1875 between historic adversaries, the Ojibwe, who had come down the St. Croix River (*Menominikeshi Zibii,* or Ricebird River), and the Dakota, who had settled for the season at the easternmost tip of land on the north shore of the Mississippi River (*Wa-Kpá Tan-Ka,* or Large River). The Ojibwe greatly overwhelmed the much smaller Dakota settlements. When Europeans later arrived in the region, the Ojibwe were living in small encampments along the lower western shores of the lake.

Although trappers and surveyors had been passing through the St. Croix Valley since the seventeenth century, the first European settlers along this shore were Mark and Mary Wright, who had chosen to emigrate from Yorkshire, England, and made their way through Canada to the St. Lawrence River and then through the Great Lakes to Chicago. They traveled west to Galena on the Mississippi and came north upriver by steamboat in 1832 and disembarked at Prescott, Wisconsin, across the lake. They crossed the St. Croix and built a cabin on the peninsula.

A few years passed before a new neighbor, Joseph Monjeau (Mozhoe), built a cabin nearby in 1838. He was quickly followed by Levi Hertzell (Hurtsill) and Oscar Burris, who in 1839 opened a combined cabin and mercantile store and had a successful trade with river travelers, French trappers, the Ojibwe, and the Dakota. In 1840, the partners secured the right to open the first post office territory outside of Fort Snelling, Hertzell serving as postmaster.

In the same year that Hertzell and Burris were opening their mercantile operation, the now famous trapper and Dakota interpreter at Fort Snelling Philander Prescott opened a trading post across the St. Croix at a site that would later be named for him. What is less well known is that he and his Dakota wife, Nah-he-no-wenah ("Spirit of the Moon"), who had taken the English name Mary, built a house on the opposite bank and surely traded with and sold to Hertzell and Burris.

David Hone arrived in 1843 as a representative of the thirteen partners of the Marine Mill Company and commissioned the Union Hotel, the first frame building on the point and by all accounts a large and handsome building, in expectation of a quickly growing town. That same year the first of many circuit ministers, the Rev. Joseph Hurlbut, preached as a guest at Point Douglas. The Rev. W. T. Boutwell stopped to preach in the town in 1844. William Dibble came to the small village in

Ferry between Point Douglas and Prescott, c1900

1845; Ephraim Whitaker, in 1846; and Martin Leavitt and Simon Shingledecker, in 1847.

In 1849, the first year of the new Minnesota Territory, Hertzell, Burris, and Hone platted the new village of Point Douglas, named in honor of Senator Stephen Douglas, who had been critical to the successful creation of the new Minnesota Territory. By this time the settlement had several hotels, warehouses, and shops and a population of nearly two hundred, and Hertzell and Burris's mercantile business had become the largest in the county, leading St. Paul's *Minnesota Chronicle and Register* to declare in 1850 that Point Douglas "would soon become among the most prominent settlements of the Territory." Burris may well have found the new state of affairs too civilized for his taste: he left for California late in that same year.

The Valley School was built in 1850, the same year that Congress approved funds to construct four roads in the territory, two of which started at Point Douglas. One road went north through Dakotah (later named Stillwater), and the other, through St. Paul and up the Minnesota River to Fort Ripley. The Stillwater road was later moved a quarter mile inland; County Road 21, known as the St. Croix Trail, follows much of its route.

The thriving community of Point Douglas then had nearly twenty houses, had built a second ferry line running to Hastings, and had become a thriving lumbering center, receiving rafts of logs floated down the St. Croix to the busy town sawmills. But in that very fact lay the beginning of the end of Point Douglas, for lumbering began to fade as the supply of big trees diminished. Worse, the town's rivals across the river, Prescott and Hastings, were becoming the predominant ports of call for steamboats coming up- and downstream, bypassing Point Douglas in favor of improved levees and more modern warehouses.

The demise of Point Douglas was hastened by the arrival of the railroad in Hastings in 1868, a full ten years before Point Douglas would secure a line on its side of the river. By the time the Chicago, Milwaukee and St. Paul Railroad had built a station and laid track in 1879 through Point Douglas heading up toward Stillwater, the beginning of the end was already apparent. The population of Point Douglas dwindled as laborers moved on for better opportunities or owners abandoned failing businesses. Houses were left vacant and commercial buildings allowed to deteriorate.

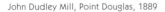
John Dudley Mill, Point Douglas, 1889

The routing of the rail line through the middle of Point Douglas destroyed much of its character and hastened the retiring of its commercial district. Entire houses and shop buildings were moved up the steep bluffs and resettled on farmlands as residences and storehouses. By the turn of the twentieth century, only a few houses were still standing; the post office was a shuttered ruin.

A continuous reworking of Highway 10 and postwar housing development spelled the final demise of all that remained of the town of Point Douglas. Only the Valley schoolhouse is still standing on its original site along present-day St. Croix Trail. The remaining buildings were moved to private properties after being carefully photographed onsite for the historical record.

Point Douglas, c1900

DENMARK TOWNSHIP: FARMS, FORESTS, AND ORCHARDS

Denmark Township, named after several townships back in New York and Maine from where a large number of settlers had emigrated, was incorporated in 1858. Many large and successful farms had been established on the upper reaches beyond Point Douglas over the previous decades. Wheat from the northern end of the township had become the predominant crop, and the grain was carted north to mills in Afton, which was much closer than Point Douglas.

In the years after the Civil War, several more schools soon dotted the township. The Point Douglas Grange No. 490 was built a decade later, in 1874, a demonstration of the success and cooperative nature of the township's active farming community. The population continued to grow in the township, and a second post office was installed in the late 1870s and enlarged again at the turn of the century. A town hall was built in 1900 and still stands on its original site.

Some miles up the government road from the flourishing community of Point Douglas was the village of Basswood Grove, which had a school, a church, a store, and several small farm holdings, all surrounded by the larger wheat farms of the township. The heart of Basswood Grove can still be found on the old government road, now the St. Croix Trail, between 80th and 87th streets, where St. Mary's Episcopal Church and cemetery were established in 1863.

 LOCAL RESOURCES

Denmark Township
14008 90th Street South
Hastings, MN 55033
651-436-1704
www.denmarktownship.org

Denmark Township Historical Society
c/o Mavis Voigt
612-823-4934
rmvoigt@usfamily.net
www.dthsmn.org

St. Mary's Episcopal Church Basswood Grove
8435 St. Croix Trail South
Hastings, MN 55033
651-436-1872
www.stmaryschurch.us

continues

Carpenter St. Croix Nature Center
12805 St. Croix Trail South
Hastings, MN 55033
651-437-4359
www.carpenternaturecenter.org

Afton State Park
6959 Peller Avenue South
Hastings, MN 55033
651-436-5391
www.dnr.state.mn.us/state_parks/afton

See Hastings and Nininger for lodging options.

POINT DOUGLAS AND DENMARK TOWNSHIP TOUR

See map on p. 39.

"NR" indicates National Register properties.

1. LEAVITT CEMETERY (EST. C. 1860)
Highway 10 east of County Road 21 (St. Croix Trail South)

One hundred sixty-five burials on land once owned by Martin Leavitt of Point Douglas. Small parking area adjacent to the roadway on the north side of the cemetery. Open dawn to dusk.

2. VILLAGE OF POINT DOUGLAS (DEMOLISHED, FIRST SETTLEMENT 1830s)
Highway 10 and County Road 21

Virtually none of the Point Douglas settlement remains after a half century of road realignment and demolition. All property on the point is now privately owned.

3. VALLEY SCHOOL (1852, ON ORIGINAL SITE)
County Road 21 just north of intersection with Highway 10

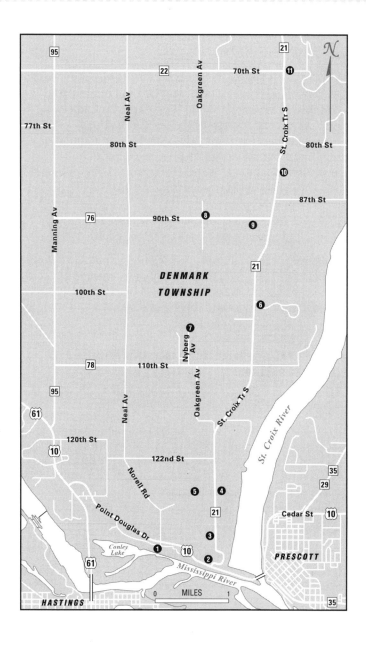

4. CARPENTER ST. CROIX VALLEY NATURE CENTER
12805 St. Croix Trail South

On the bluffs above the St. Croix, Carpenter Nature Center originated as an estate of architectural masterpieces commissioned during the 1940s by Thomas Carpenter, president of the Sperry Office Furniture Company, and his wife, Edna. The Carpenters established a foundation that brought their dream of a nature center to fruition, and after their deaths in the 1970s, work began on the property, with the center opening in 1981.

5. POINT DOUGLAS (JOHNSON) CEMETERY (EST. 1855)
Across the highway from Carpenter Nature Center

Known to hold thirty-one burials, though many are now unmarked.

6. ST. CROIX REGIONAL BLUFFS PARK
10191 St. Croix Trail South

7. LOST VALLEY PRAIRIE SCIENTIFIC AND WILDLIFE AREA (MINNESOTA DNR)
From County Road 78 (110th Street South) go north on Nyberg Avenue South, park at end of road

An intact and priceless swath of original prairie, this 320-acre tract of land was once part of Mark and Mary Wright's farm. Acquired with the help of the township, the county, and the Trust for Public Land, Lost Valley SNA's prairielands are now under the care of the Minnesota Department of Natural Resources. The SNA's footpaths are accessible and open to the public.

8. DENMARK TOWNSHIP HALL (1900, ON ORIGINAL SITE)
14008 90th Street South

9. WRIGHT/GREENWOOD CEMETERY (EST. 1888)

St. Croix Trail South on west side, just south of 90th Street

Established on land donated by Point Douglas's first settlers, Mark and Mary Wright. All sixty-five burials are descendants of the Wrights.

10. ST. MARY'S EPISCOPAL CHURCH AND CEMETERY, BASSWOOD GROVE (EST. 1860s)

8435 St. Croix Trail South (between 80th and 87th Streets)

The cemetery holds about three hundred burials.

11. AFTON STATE PARK

County Road 21 and County Highway 22

One of the region's most beloved state parks for its beauty in all seasons. Hiking trails (many accessible) wind through oak savannas and prairie grasslands, into deep ravines, and atop bluffs overlooking the St. Croix River.

AFTON TOWNSHIP

Afton sits on the Minnesota shore where the St. Croix River begins to widen into Lake St. Croix. Afton Township comprises the village and the beautiful valleys and farmlands to the west that proved irresistible to a diverse community of settlers.

This broadening of the St. Croix River was known to the Dakota as *Ho-Ġań O-Wań-Ka Kin,* and to the Ojibwe as *Gegoshugahmote,* both names translating as the Place Where the Fish Come. These names reference a great body of deep water where fish rest until the arrival of the spawning season.

The district's first known European settlers were the French Canadian family members of voyageur and trader Gaspare Bruce, who having originally settled in the far north on the Red River near the Canadian border relocated to the St. Croix in 1837. He settled at the mouth of a fast-flowing creek, later to be named Bolles Creek for the miller who settled upstream. Jean-Baptiste Fournier (alternately, Tournier) joined them a few years later, and the small group of settlers raised garden crops. More settlers, the majority from New England states— New York, Maine, and Pennsylvania—or from the British Isles, found their way to the shore near the creek for its good waterpower, the availability of rich farmlands on the slopes above the river, and the river itself, which permitted shipping of lumber and goods and the arrival of passengers. Lemuel Bolles arrived in 1838 to settle up the creek, building a small flour mill and a grindstone quarry.

The government road was built north from Point Douglas into Afton in 1847, and surveying continued north toward Superior and Duluth after 1850. The new road permitted an excellent alternative to river shipping and trade, and the first grist mill north of Prairie du Chien, Wisconsin, was built by Erastus Bolles, Lemuel's nephew. The road allowed him to receive grain and ship flour from his new grist mill throughout the year.

AFTON VILLAGE

Afton Village was surveyed and platted in 1855 and organized in 1858, an effort managed by the Haskell, Getchell, and Thomas families. The village, though tiny (six blocks wide and ten blocks long), was given a lovely siting on the shore of Lake St. Croix and included a plot of land set aside for a cemetery. Lemuel Bolles prevailed in giving the new village the name of his own business, Milton Mills, which many found more sophisticated than the colloquial Catfish Bar, commemorating the large sandbar that permitted cattle and horses to ford the river when water levels in the lake were low.

Within a few years, the Getchells persuaded the townsfolk to adopt the name Afton from Robert Burns's poem "Afton Waters," with its picturesque evocation of hills and valleys around wandering streams, in this case the two lovely branches of Bolles Creek that rose from springs high up the bluffs and wandered down into the village to the shore of Lake St. Croix.

Afton Village began to attract businesses and became a thriving commercial center with a hotel, a blacksmith,

Bolles family at home, Valley Creek, c1910

a fish market, and a mercantile store. Perhaps the influence of the many New Englanders and immigrants from Great Britain explains the clean, simple, but beautiful lines of many of the commercial buildings and jewel-like cottages and modest houses that were built in the village. A unique architectural contribution was the Meredith Thomas Octagon House, built in 1855 (razed 1944).

The Rev. Simon Putnam was the first pastor to serve at the new Congregational Church of Afton, established in 1858 with a parish of thirteen members. A public school was organized in Afton Village, classes taking place in Rev. Putnam's kitchen until a schoolhouse could be built. The Rev. Putnam enlisted as a chaplain in the Third Minnesota Regiment and died of his war wounds shortly after the surrender at Appomattox in 1864.

HAMLET OF VALLEY CREEK

This tiny community, at a crossroads two miles up the creek from Afton, was where Lemuel and Erastus Bolles built their mills. There was a store and a blacksmithing shop for the manufacturing of tools and for fine metalworking. Though the hamlet remained apart from the bustling village down on the lakeshore, those who settled there prospered. While it never incorporated as a village, post–Civil War growth finally prompted the building of a school and a town hall and the settlement of new neighbors.

John William Boxell, who arrived at Valley Creek in 1854, ran a private school for some years a mile west of the community. Boxell was also the driving force behind horticulture in the district, planting some of Minnesota's first orchards and vineyards, teaching and experimenting with fruit and berry culture on his famed Boxell Premium Farms, and in time becoming the state chair of the fruit and berry committee of the Minnesota Horticultural Society. Later, when lumber failed the township as a commercial opportunity, Boxell's efforts would figuratively bear fruit in the formation of the Afton Berry Association.

In all, some twenty houses were built up in Valley Creek before and after the Civil War, and a significant number of them were substantial and handsome by all accounts, a quite different environment from the village of modest cottages and houses down the hill in Afton.

HAMLET OF SOUTH AFTON

This outlier of Afton Village, never formally incorporated as a village, was in the post–Civil War years largely commercial, becoming a major milling district with elevators, warehouses, and stores. A rope ferry was also established to enable transport across to the Wisconsin shore. The present-day River Road South, which turns off the St. Croix Trail at the south end of Afton, was the main thoroughfare for the mills and warehouses and also the route of the Chicago, Milwaukee and St. Paul Railroad. All traces of this industrial district are now gone, replaced by residential structures.

HAMLET OF SWEDE HILL

Though never incorporated as a village, Swede Hill was settled after the Civil War by Swedish immigrants, drawn by enthusiastic correspondence from earlier settlers, chose land on the rocky hilltops to the southwest of Afton. The region reminded them of home, and they were among the strongest proponents of the post–lumber era move to truck farming, largely berry and garden crops.

THE CIVIL WAR YEARS AND BEYOND

Afton Township easily mustered enough volunteers, leaving behind shops, mills, and farms, to fill out the requested township rolls, and the soldiers were subsequently sorted out to a number of different Minnesota regiments. Edward Cox of Swede Hill, eventually rising to the rank of general, was known to have drilled Afton volunteers for the Third Minnesota Regiment in his kitchen. Later, the Afton Village city park was used as a parade ground. At the time of the first call-up, a home relief society was formed to look after and provide for the families of the enlisted.

By the end of the Civil War, the township had not only a substantial population base of transplanted Yankees, Brits, Irish, Scots, and French but also large groups of Germans and Swedes and not a few Swiss. Distinctive districts began to form, some of which became incorporated as villages in their own right but most being absorbed into the township government, retaining their unique stories in their names.

The cornerstone of one of the state's first high schools, the new, advanced, and very handsome St. Croix Academy, was laid by the Free Masons at a site on the main street at the north end of Afton Village in 1868. The building stood three stories high, was built of brick and stone, and was topped with a bell tower;

St. Croix Academy, Afton, built 1868

the interior was finished out in oak and black walnut. A library was presented to the school by the village, and pianos and organs were furnished for the music room. The basement, besides being used for storage and fuel, provided a gymnasium where young men were instructed in the fine points of boxing. Instruction was offered in the classics and higher English, vocal and instrumental music, and German.

The township was very enthusiastic about the new school. One of the first students at the academy was C. E. Bolles, Erastus's son, and over 130 others signed on in the first term. But enrollment began to fall off after the first decade, and by 1884 the academy had closed. The building and its campus were purchased by Rev. P. Duborg, who presented the property to the Evangelical Lutheran Joint Synod of Ohio in hopes of receiving backing for a new theological seminary. The seminary lasted fewer than ten years, moving to St. Paul in 1893, at which time the building was acquired by School District No. 24.

The Chicago, Milwaukee and St. Paul Railroad built a station and laid track in 1879 from Point Douglas through Afton Village, heading up toward Stillwater. The population of Afton Township was numbered at 925, about half American born, half German and Swedish immigrants.

Minnesota's fifth governor, William Rainey Marshall (1866–70), retired to the St. Croix and built an exceptionally beautiful and elegant mansion near the Valley Creek crossroads. Devising a true showplace, Marshall built a grand house in the style of southern plantation houses, complete with great pillars supporting a second-story portico under which carriages could sweep through on a circular drive.

Louis Lovell May established one of the first commercial nurseries in the state in 1899, covering some 250 acres up in Valley Creek, and bought Marshall's mansion in 1900, joining the Valley Creek community. By now the distinctive boundaries between the many small incorporated and unincorporated villages was blurring, and services were increasingly consolidated in Afton Village as the main commercial center. A sign of the times was the closing of the Valley Creek post office in 1901.

The Mays squandered much of their fortune through unfortunate stock and currency speculation, and the entire business and house were lost to the banks. It may have been in the decades afterward that the great house was razed. The acreage of the nursery was fostered by later owners who bought the site in 1931 and worked to keep the many varieties of plants and shrubbery thriving, but over the years the L. L. May Nursery faded into Afton's past.

The Afton Fruit and Farm Produce Association, a cooperative, was established in 1914 and became a major employer of farm hands and their families in the production of strawberries, gooseberries, currants, raspberries, blackberries, and orchard fruits. The produce was picked, crated, delivered to the Afton Berry Market (fondly called "The Shed"), and then distributed to buyers and markets in St. Paul.

Afton soon settled into a quiet pattern of self-sufficiency and gentle architectural decline. Most needed services were to be found along the village main street unless a medical emergency dictated a rare trip up to Stillwater or into St. Paul. The quiet side streets and the city park provided an ideal life on the river, and if the houses were gradually falling into some disrepair, the tax base was still sufficient to provide the basic municipal services.

The stores entertained summer visitors and in winter supplied the residents with necessities. The Cushing Hotel became, in time, the Afton House Inn and was regularly patronized by guests from many towns up and down the river and well beyond, being the only lodging between Hastings and Stillwater.

After the end of Prohibition, Harold Lind turned his confectionary store on the main street into Lerk's Bar and Grill, borrowing his childhood nickname (which means "onion" in Swedish). Selma's Ice Cream Parlor (and variously also beer and sandwich tavern, bait shop, and post office) remains a popular draw three seasons out of four, though its fate is now uncertain.

Once discovered again by city day-trippers, houseboat owners, heritage travelers, and seekers of new land on which to build homes, Afton has kept up with the times without sacrificing the elements of its history. Road names have been changed to meet county and state standards, and a great many of the oldest commercial and residential structures are still in Afton proper but no longer on their original sites. The village is a delight, and the outlying districts such as Valley Creek are designated to be of national historic value.

Much of the historic riverfront is now a modern harbor for a sizeable marina, and all vestiges of historic commercial and residential structures are gone. The Afton Historical Society, its fine museum, and the village's many popular businesses draw thousands of visitors every year, however, who stop to shop or eat or simply to admire the tiny neat streets and well-cared-for houses.

 **LOCAL RESOURCES**

City of Afton Business Association and Chamber of Commerce
651-436-8883
kathy@aftonhouseinn.com
www.aftonmnarea.com

Afton Historical Society
3165 St. Croix Trail South
Afton, MN 55001
651-436-3500
scriv@pressenter.com
www.pressenter.com/~aftnhist
Open Wednesdays, 1:00 to 8:00 p.m., throughout the year (weather permitting) and Sundays, 1:00 to 4:00 p.m., mid-May to mid-October. Tours by appointment.

continues

Belwin Conservancy and Outdoor Education Laboratory
1553 Stagecoach Trail South
Afton, MN 55001
651-436-5189
www.belwin.org

🛏 LODGING OPTIONS

Historic Afton House Inn and Afton-Hudson Cruise Lines
3291 St. Croix Trail South
Afton, MN 55001
651-436-8883 or 877-436-8883
info@aftonhouseinn.com
www.aftonhouseinn.com
www.stcroixrivercruises.com

Afton's Mulberry Pond Bed and Breakfast
3786 River Road South
Afton, MN 55001
651-436-8086

See also Hastings and Nininger, Hudson, and Stillwater.

AFTON TOWNSHIP TOUR

See map on p. 53.

See map on p. 53.

Afton Village proper is fewer than seven blocks long and, in most places, one block wide on each side of County Road 21, the St. Croix Trail, which is the village's de facto Main Street. Afton streets start and stop without warning despite what the street atlas tells you. Many thoroughfares on the map do not exist or are not on the map and *do* exist, and Afton streets have had their names changed repeatedly over the decades as the city, township, county, and state have overlaid mandates for road naming and the better access of emergency vehicles.

If you come during the week or during the winter season, the serene pace of the village is a rest for the mind. Arrive on the weekend from midspring to late autumn and you will be joined by a thousand of your closest friends (an astonishing number of them on motorcycles), and lots of them will be driving much faster than you are.

Of the four National Register properties in Afton Township, only one is easily viewable and open to the public: the Afton House Inn, originally built as the Cushing Hotel in 1867 to offer lodgings for railroad workers, lumbermen, and commercial travelers. The remaining three properties, the Erastus Bolles House (1856; 1741 Stagecoach Trail), the Silas Geer House (c. 1860; 1872 Stagecoach Trail), and the Newington Gilbert House (1864; 1678 Stagecoach Trail), are all private residences up in Valley Creek and well hidden behind shrubbery, which affords the owners some privacy. None of the houses are open for tours.

There have been some real losses. Much of the historic riverfront is now a modern harbor for a sizeable marina, and all vestiges of historic commercial and residential structures are gone. Also, a great many of the oldest commercial and residential structures are still in Afton proper but no longer on their original sites.

The village is, however, very aware of its important story, and the Afton Historical Society has developed some exceptionally detailed walking and driving tours around the village and the outlying districts such as Valley Creek. These tours, with beautiful graphics, are among the best heritage tourism documents produced by any of Minnesota's local historical societies.

Four tours are available as PDFs at www.pressenter. com/~aftnhist and can also be picked up from the Afton House Inn—"Village Walking Tour," "Military Road Tour," "Valley Creek Tour," and the "South Afton and Swede Hill Tour." A historical marker honoring the Bolles Mill site was installed by the Minnesota Historical Society just north of the intersection of St. Croix Trail and Stagecoach Road.

MOUNT HOPE CEMETERY, AFTON VILLAGE
From Afton Boulevard north out of Afton Village, take the second left onto Pennington, and bear right on a steep incline up 34th Street. Park at the wayside by the cemetery entrance.

The Mount Hope Cemetery is the oldest burial ground in Afton (first burial in 1854, last in 1892). Four Civil War markers, including for the Rev. Simon Putnam, chaplain to the Third Minnesota Regiment, and his son, Simon, who both died of their wounds at the end of the Civil War. There may be as many as sixty additional unmarked graves. Once considered one of Minnesota's most endangered properties, Mount Hope is now under the care of dedicated volunteer preservationists.

ST. PAULUS LUTHERAN CEMETERY, AFTON VILLAGE
Turn off from the village main street on 31st Street and park behind Mudslinger Pottery.

This small but lovely burial ground was dedicated in the 1880s, abandoned in the 1940s, and restored in the late 1980s by a scout troop. It is now maintained by the City of Afton.

AFTON TOWNSHIP HALL, VALLEY CREEK
Two miles north of Afton on Stagecoach Trail

This lovely and picturesque structure is the only remaining nonresidential building in Valley Creek.

THE BELWIN CONSERVANCY AND OUTDOOR NATURE LAB, VALLEY CREEK
Located just beyond the intersection of Stagecoach Trail and 15th Street

This magnificent 1,300-acre preserve was a gift of retired General Mills chairman Charles H. Bell and wife Lucy Winton Bell to the Belwin Foundation to establish a nonprofit open-air nature center, an environmental research center, and a recreational site for area youth.

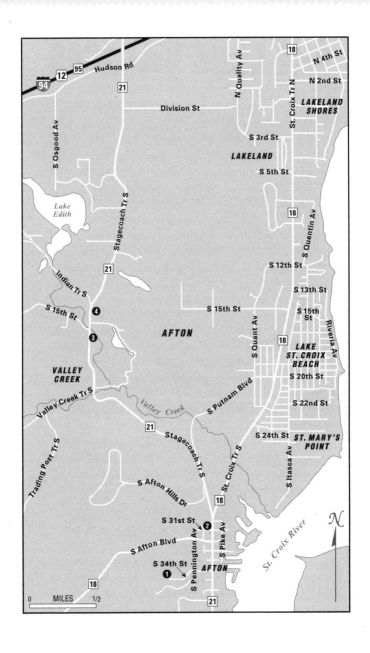

AFTON TOWNSHIP

N 4th St
18
N 2nd St
St. Croix Tr N
LAKELAND SHORES
N Quality Av
Hudson Rd
12
95
94
21
Division St
S 3rd St
S Osgood Av
LAKELAND
S 5th St
Stagecoach Tr S
Lake Edith
18
S Quentin Av
21
S 12th St
Indian Tr S
S 13th St
S 15th St
S 15th St
4
S 15th St
AFTON
Riverla Av
3
18
LAKE ST. CROIX BEACH
S Quant Av
VALLEY CREEK
S 20th St
Valley Creek
S 22nd St
Valley Creek Tr S
S Putnam Blvd
S 24th St
ST. MARY'S POINT
21
S Itasca Av
Stagecoach Tr S
Trading Post Tr S
St. Croix Tr S
18
N
S Afton Hills Dr
S 31st St
2
St. Croix River
S Afton Blvd
S Pennington Av
S Pike Av
S 34th St
1
AFTON
18
21

0   MILES   1/2

THE LAKE VILLAGES

The communities on the west shore of Lake St. Croix all had early European settlements in the nineteenth century, but it wasn't until after 1900 that folks wanting to escape the urban heat and close quarters of the city began looking for land on which to build small summer cabins with fresh, healthy air within a day's ride from St. Paul.

Building started slowly down the lakeshore in the mid-1920s, as small cottages began to dot the platted village sites near 1880s farmhouses that at the time offered just enough ground for a vegetable garden. In the post–World War II years, building began in earnest, but the size of the houses remained modest. This uniformity of postwar year-round residences characterizes the four incorporated villages of St. Mary's Point, Lake St. Croix Beach, Lakeland Shores, and Lakeland, which are strung from south to north without visible boundaries, with the St. Croix Trail (now County Road 18) running through as the main thoroughfare. The old Chicago, Milwaukee and St. Paul Railroad right-of-way passes through all these communities, now hidden under paved streets.

Today, the city of Lakeland virtually surrounds Lakeland Shores and ducks under the old Hudson Road— now Interstate 94 where it crosses over into Wisconsin— and reveals some hidden secrets.

ST. MARY'S POINT

This village, on a point of land at the north end of Afton Township, was named by a traveling Jesuit missionary. The district's first known settlers were the French Canadian traders Gaspare Bruce and Jean-Baptiste Fournier, who, in 1837 on the point of land between Lake St. Croix and what became known as Bolles Creek, installed

their Dakota wives and families. The small group of settlers raised garden crops.

Bruce sold his claim in March 1844 to Henry Sibley,
who was then an agent for the American Fur Company,
and Sibley in turn traded it in July of that year to Joseph
R. Brown. Brown sold the western and south sections
of the farm to Lemuel Bolles, who by 1846 had the first
flouring mill on the creek and baptized the flowing
stream with his name.

Land sales in the valley had opened in 1848, but the
small village wasn't to be platted until nearly a decade
later. The first land plats were sited on the point by
James Carr and Thomas Coleman in 1855 and the village
incorporation promoted by Coleman in 1857.

There was little success in drawing speculators, and
the land was replatted by St. Paul investors Alexander
Cathcart and William Rainey Marshall. It was an ambitious design, a prospective industrial town with a steamboat landing along the entire shoreline to accommodate
the shipping barges and tourist boats that would surely
come. Several houses *were* built at St. Mary's Point, and
partners from Philadelphia built a sawmill out on the
point itself. The new mill burnt within a few months
of its construction, however, and the little settlement
lasted less than a year.

By the early 1880s St. Mary's Point was virtually
abandoned, with the exception of the Chicago, Milwaukee and St. Paul Railroad, which ran north-south from
Point Douglas to Stillwater. Meanwhile, W. R. Marshall
had served (and survived) as an officer of the Seventh
Minnesota Voluntary Regiment during the Civil War
and, within a year after discharge, joined the Republican Party and served as Minnesota's fifth governor from
1866 to 1870.

With the renewed interest in the fresh air of the
river so close to St. Paul, John Humbird, a lumber and
railroad tycoon, bought forty acres of shoreline in St.
Mary's Point in 1910 and built four summer homes for
his four daughters and their families.

Residential building and summer resort development continued through the two world wars, with the Village of St. Mary's Point incorporating in 1951 and a city hall being built in 1958. City status came in 1976 with the name and original platted boundaries of St. Mary's Point much as they were 150 years ago.

LAKE ST. CROIX BEACH

This tiny hamlet was the last of the Lake St. Croix west shore sites to develop, remaining for a very long time a rural farming community contained inside the boundaries of Afton Township.

As with the neighboring villages, tourism found Lake St. Croix Beach after 1900. The *St. Paul Daily News* bought a 300-acre parcel with shoreline and began to promote affordable cottage lots as part of its subscription drives. The lots were, by any stretch of the buyers' imaginations, modest. Nevertheless, hundreds of the 20-by-100-foot lots were sold steadily for $10 down and $2.50 a month. Tiny summer cottages sprang up like daisies. And if lot owners couldn't afford to build just then, they would come to Lake St. Croix Beach, picnic on their property, and launch boats or go for a swim on the village beach.

The platted town was built around, indeed surrounded, the summer home of famed Stillwater lumber baron George Atwood, who held thirty acres on the lake for his house on stilts, which he had dubbed the Anchorage. Within a decade of the *St. Paul Daily News*'s development efforts, which attracted builders of summer cottages on some one hundred platted blocks, Atwood sold his lakeshore home to the St. Paul Automobile Club as a summer clubhouse with all the expected amenities such as boating, fishing, and swimming.

Accusing Washington County of having failed to adequately maintain the roads necessary for easy travel of the newfangled automobiles being used by city dwellers to travel out to the river, the SPAC moved to better rail, trolley, and road access at White Bear Lake in 1912. The old clubhouse became the Lake St. Croix Beach Property Owners' Association, sponsored by the *Daily News,* a place to gather, hold dances, and generally socialize.

The building lasted just until the post–World War II years, coming down in 1950. The Depression had already stripped property away from cottage owners and spelled the demise of the *Daily News* itself in 1938. But the village began to see a renewed interest in summer cottagers after incorporation in 1952. By the time Lake St. Croix Beach became a city in 1974, many of the small summer homes had been retrofitted for year-around living.

LAKELAND SHORES

Like Lake St. Croix Beach, Lakeland Shores was once a large single farm owned by the William and Mary Jones family; it is surrounded by the city of Lakeland. The Joneses had their land surveyed in the 1940s for 100- and 150-foot lots along the riverfront on present-day Lakeland Shores Road, the old Chicago, Milwaukee and St. Paul Railroad right-of-way. The 443-acre community, which achieved city status in 1974, is entirely residential.

LAKELAND

This community, which surrounds Lakeland Shores on the west and north, extends under and beyond the Old Hudson Road, now Interstate 94.

As with St. Mary's Point, the shoreline of Lake St. Croix had a small settlement of French Canadian and Native American families subsisting on fishing, trading, and garden drops in the 1840s. The first of the European settlers to claim land was Henry W. Crosby, who in 1842 laid out a farm on land that was situated for trade and commerce with the village of Hudson across the river. Moses Perin (Perrin), one of the many French Canadians making their way down the St. Croix Valley, arrived six years later and began a ferry service around which he staked claim to land, platted the town, and built several structures. Perin gave the city a portion of his own land on which to establish the Lakeland Cemetery in 1854 as a public burial ground.

One of the first of the new residents to arrive was John Oliver, who had a distinguished history as an officer in the British navy and a harbor pilot in Boston Bay. Oliver took over operation of the Lakeland ferry and built a large, handsome farming estate on the hill above. Within a few years, the town had a wagon-making shop, a post office, a mercantile store, a saloon, a doctor, and a lawyer, the last three arriving nearly simultaneously in happy serendipity.

By 1858, there were a total of fourteen residential dwellings, shops, churches, and hotels in the business district known familiarly as Shanghai Cooley (coulee), named for the town postmaster's hobby of raising Shanghai chickens, an exotic breed of fowl known for their great size and quantity of eggs.

Lakeland School, 1895

A boat building company was established in 1871. Lakeland was replatted to include a large public square and a riverside depot in anticipation of the arrival of the St. Paul and Milwaukee railroad. But in a few years the dream had faded. The need for more reliable transport for the new automobile, as much as for horse-drawn carts, across Lake St. Croix to Hudson dictated that a new wooden toll bridge be built in 1913, connecting to a long natural dike in the Hudson Harbor. Lakeland was still a quiet lakeside town through the 1950s, when the Village of Lakeland was incorporated.

Today, the Shanghai Cooley ravine lies almost entirely under the mass of the Interstate 94 overhead roadbed and bridge abutments. The village is filled with houses tiny and large, with several of notable historic distinction. And though visitors can remain on the St. Croix Trail (County Road 18) to head north, just for sheer delight they also have the pleasant prospect of becoming wholly lost amongst the streets of Lakeland clustered near the lakeshore, all enjoying the distinction of starting with the letter Q, rare enough in the English language. Thus, Quixote, Quinnell, Quinimore, Quinlan, Quentin, Queenan, Quehl, Quant, Quamwell, and Quality avenues make their steady march from the shore west to the Stagecoach Trail (County Road 21), the old Point Douglas–Superior government road.

ⓘ LOCAL RESOURCES

City of Lakeland
690 Quinnell Avenue North
Lakeland, MN 55043
651-436-4430
cityoflakeland@comcast.net
http://lakelandmn.com/History.htm
Open Monday thru Friday, 9:00 a.m. to noon, or by appointment.

See Afton, Stillwater, Hastings, and Hudson for lodging options.

THE LAKE VILLAGES TOUR

See map on p. 61.

"NR" indicates National Register properties.

St. Mary's Point and Lake St. Croix Beach

1. CHURCH OF ST. FRANCIS OF ASSISI
13th Street South at Riviera Avenue, Lake St. Croix Beach

Built in an exceptionally beautiful adobe mission style, of simple, clean lines. Cornerstone laid in 1938 by Archbishop John Murray. Completed 1939, now retained as a chapel. New church built in replication of the old, in mission style on exterior and interior using white stucco, wood ceilings, and beams. A graceful marble statue of St. Francis is found on the grounds above the lake framed in a glass grotto, beyond which the lake can be seen.

Lakeland Shores and Lakeland

There are three National Register properties in Lakeland, of which two—the John Cyphers House and the Captain John Oliver estate—are easily viewed. The Mitchell Jackson Farmhouse, on the far side of the Lakeland district, is a privately owned property up a long wooded drive and is not open to the public.

2. LAKEVIEW CEMETERY (1854)
8th Street North at Queenan Avenue North, Lakeland

This cemetery was dedicated on land given to the newly platted village of Lakeland by Moses Perin (Perrin) as a public burying ground. Over 800 burials.

3. JOHN T. CYPHERS HOUSE (C. 1858, NR)
661 Quinnell Avenue North, Lakeland

A small cottage with thick exterior walls of "grout," an early concrete construction material made of lime, sand,

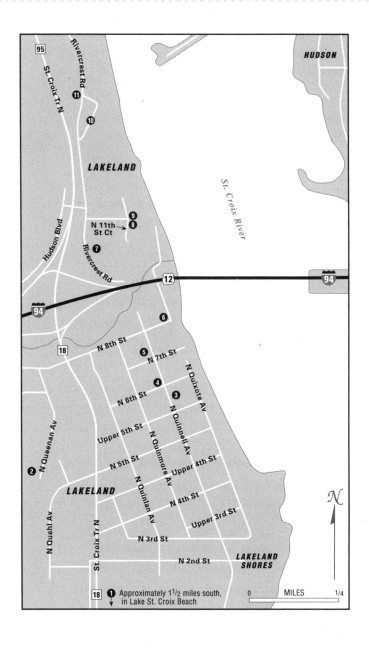

HUDSON

95

Rivercrest Rd

St. Croix Tr N

11

10

LAKELAND

St. Croix River

Hudson Blvd

9
8
N 11th
St Ct

Rivercrest Rd

7

12

94

94

18

6

N 8th St

5
N 7th St

N Quixote Av

4

N 6th St

3

N Quinnell Av

Upper 5th St

N Quinmore Av

N Queenan Av

N 5th St

Upper 4th St

2

LAKELAND

N Quinlan Av

N 4th St

Upper 3rd St

N Quehl Av

St. Croix Tr N

N 3rd St

N 2nd St

LAKELAND
SHORES

N

18

1 Approximately 1½ miles south,
in Lake St. Croix Beach

0   MILES   1/4

mud, and gravel. Cyphers built the house after reading about the concept in an 1855 edition of St. Paul's *Pioneer Press*. Cyphers poured the mixture into two-foot-thick frames to form the walls.

4. LAKELAND CITY HALL (1869)
690 Quinnell Avenue North, Lakeland

Built as the First Baptist Church in an octagon shape, possibly from a catalog design. Remodeled as a two-room schoolhouse in the late 1940s; remodeled again in 1986 with an addition for use as Lakeland City Hall.

5. CHURCH, NOW RESIDENCE (N. D.)
768 Quinnell Avenue North, Lakeland

6. STAPLES (?) HOUSE (C. 1880)
8th Street North at Quixote Avenue North, Lakeland

7. FARMHOUSE AND BARN (C. 1880)
Rivercrest Road North, Lakeland (north of Interstate 94)

8. RESIDENCE (C. 1880)

9. RESIDENCE (C. 1880)
11th Street Court North, Lakeland (north of Interstate 94)

10. OLD TOLL BRIDGE ROAD (C. 1848)

This lane once led down to the ferry established by Moses Perin (Perrin) in 1848 and run by Captain John Oliver for ten years.

11. CAPTAIN JOHN OLIVER HOUSE (1849, NR)
1544 Rivercrest Road, Lakeland (north of Interstate 94)

Greek Revival frame residence on a farming estate built in 1849 for Captain John Oliver, a British naval officer, early Lakeland settler, and St. Croix River ferry operator.

BAYPORT

Present-day Bayport comprises what once were three small settlements strung out below Dakotah (Stillwater), platted as Baytown, Bangor, and Middletown. All three were scooped up into the new name of South Stillwater, later changed to Bayport, with the township retaining its original name of Baytown.

Among the names we find of the earliest European settlers in this district, many are, again, French Canadian. Pierre "Pig's Eye" Parrant—so named for his unfortunate appearance and unsettling social manners— arrived from St. Paul around 1840 to make a land claim and to manage Norman Kittson's American Fur Company trading post, housed in a cabin Kittson had built out on a spit of land. By 1842, Parrant's claim was sold to Joseph Renshaw Brown of Stillwater (under some duress, as the sheriff was asked to be in attendance), and Parrant, simultaneously, left the country.

François Bruce, a trader in the employ of the American Fur Company and most probably family to the fur trader Gaspare Bruce—who settled farther down the shore by the estuary of Bolles Creek at Afton—arrived the same year Parrant left and built a blockhouse near the lakeshore on present-day Central Avenue. Fellow trader and riverboat pilot of some twenty-six years Joseph "Big Joe" Perro (Perreault) settled up the hill in 1847 on the small Spring Creek, which rose from a spring-fed pond to tumble downhill and find a winding path along the lower marshlands to the lake. Both the pond and the stream would later be named for Perro.

New Englanders and arrivals from the United Kingdom followed the French Canadians to the promising shoreline, its distinctive peninsulas offering natural harbors. John Allen arrived in 1844 to farm. Socrates Nelson and David Loomis settled here in 1850.

Also arriving in 1850 were Ambrose Secrest, his wife and six children, his father, his mother, and his three brothers. They had all come upriver together on the steamer *Menominee* from Indiana, a boat that was later notorious for having carried a cholera epidemic. They squeezed in to François Bruce's vacated house, which could not have been any larger than two rooms. Within days of their arrival, Secrest's mother, father, and wife, one of his children, and two of his brothers had died.

Secrest struggled on with the help of his remaining brother to care for his five living children. He joined Joseph Perro in platting an addition in 1854 around a new flouring mill Secrest had built on Spring Creek.

Nelson and Loomis built a steam sawmill on the lakeshore in 1853 and platted Baytown in 1856 around the mill. Isaac Staples and Andrew "Jack" Short laid out the village of Bangor a little ways down the lakeshore, in honor (and high expectations) of the great lumbering town of the same name in Maine. William Holcombe, the territory's ex–lieutenant governor, platted Middle-town a ways to the north.

Baytown Township was named by Commissioner Nelson for the bay of Lake St. Croix, formed by Kittson's Point, on which the string of villages was sited. The Nelson and Loomis steam sawmill company disbanded in 1858, the same year the new township was established, and Nelson took ownership of the entirety of the Baytown property.

In that same year, Perro and Secrest donated Block 5 of their platted land as a cemetery, naming it Hazelwood. It was a sad irony that the first recorded death was Perro's son, Sylvester. In later years, they would give half of the block to the City of Stillwater for a potter's field, then the common name for the burial sites of the indigent and the unknown. A year later, in 1859, the partners donated one and a half blocks of their land to Thomas Grace, the state's new Catholic bishop recently installed in St. Paul. The new cemetery was named St. Michael's, and to this new burial ground were moved the bodies of all known Catholic dead in the Baytown and Stillwater vicinity.

The Civil War found a ready response from all of Baytown, which now also included a small lumbering village on the northwest called Oak Park, platted in 1856. Most of the young men enlisted during the first year of the war and were placed with the Eighth Minnesota Regiment at Fort Snelling. Before they were to depart to the east, however, the regiment was called to move up the Minnesota River to fight in the U.S.–Dakota War of 1862. The regiment was then sent east and south and remained until the surrender of Lee at Appomattox, which the regiment witnessed.

In the years after the war, the original plat of Baytown was purchased by Isaac Staples and Louis Torinus with the intention of rebuilding the languishing mill that had been erected by Socrates Nelson a decade earlier. But plans fell through, and the entire property was sold to the St. Croix Railway and Improvement Company, among whose partners were Staples and Torinus. The SCR&IC then bought up the Bangor and Middletown additions on either side of Baytown and looked to purchase Perro and Secrest's plat as well.

This newly cobbled collection of plats was resurveyed in 1872 and named South Stillwater. A spur line track was built running down from Stillwater, and a post office was established a year later, in 1873, housed in the offices of Torinus's new St. Croix Lumber Company, which, in addition to selling building materials and boxes, included a large cooperage for the manufacture of barrels and a large boardinghouse able to accommodate one hundred working men. Despite a devastating fire in 1876, the company rebuilt, and South Stillwater soon had other milling firms based there, including the Turnbull steam sawmill, David Tozer's South Stillwater Lumber Company, and the Herschey Lumber Company.

The Stillwater Dock Company, in which the St. Croix Lumber Company was a partner, was established in 1877 and built numerous barges and steamships. The

South Stillwater Agricultural works assembled threshing machines. A brass foundry was established, and several printing companies built their commercial plants in the new town. The St. Croix Lake Ice Company began cutting great blocks from the river for storage in sawdust until the summer came and commercial and residential kitchens alike would want ice to keep food fresh.

New settlers had been pouring into South Stillwater since the end of the Civil War, mostly Germans and Irish. They were joined by Scandinavian immigrants in the 1870s and Italians and Eastern Europeans in the 1880s. The arrival of the rail lines in 1872 had linked South Stillwater both to the city of Stillwater and to Hudson, Wisconsin, and the town became a station stop for the Chicago and Northwestern lines, which made South Stillwater (actually, the hamlet of Siegel just to the west, at present-day Osgood Avenue and 47th Street North) the junction where the rail lines diverged to either St. Paul or Stillwater.

A streetcar line following the same route arrived in 1889, but it was short lived, enduring only three years. A new streetcar venture was begun in 1905 connecting the same cities, and the ferry that had been

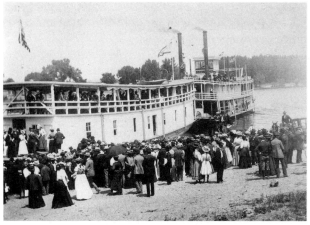

Steamer *Columbia* loading at Bayport, 1900

operating between South Stillwater and North Hudson ceased service when the Hudson toll bridge was constructed in 1913.

The timing of the toll bridge was ideal. It supported the decision of the Andersen Lumber Company, founded in 1897 in Hudson, to move across the lake to South Stillwater in 1913, where it established offices and warehouses and made use of the excellent rail service. Granted, it had to move most of its heavy machinery across the lake in the winter on thickly frozen ice, but the new bridge permitted the Andersen family to continue living in Hudson for some years. The Andersen Corporation, nationally famous producer of windows and doors, is the successor to that nineteenth-century lumber mill.

With the coming of the automobile and the frequency of rail passenger service, the streetcar lines ceased operation to South Stillwater in 1932. The Depression hit all American cities hard, and South Stillwater, which had been incorporated as the Village of Bayport in 1922, became the site of one of the federal Works Progress Administration's CCC camps, laid out almost exactly where much of the Andersen Corporation manufacturing facilities now stand.

Fred C. Andersen, president, Andersen Lumber Company, Bayport, 1924

The Andersen family, whose lumber and manufacturing company then dominated the industrial life of Bayport, were extensively involved in the well-being of the community and the quality of its civic life. The company's founder, H. J. Andersen, began sending baskets of food to impoverished families during the Depression and supported the little town in countless ways through continued donations of funds, supplies, and manpower. With the success of the Andersen Company, Bayport also prospered, and though the years of World War II were lean ones, Andersen dedicated itself to furnishing provisions for the war effort overseas and, afterward, provided jobs for returning war veterans. Postwar housing boomed, and a new hotel, the White Pine Inn, was built in 1974.

 **LOCAL RESOURCES**

City of Bayport
294 North 3rd Street
Bayport, MN 55003
651-275-4404
khuftel@ci.bayport.mn.us
http://bayport.govoffice.com
Open Monday thru Thursday, 7:30 a.m. to 5:00 p.m.

Baytown Township
4220 Osgood Avenue North
Stillwater, MN 55082
651-430-4992
www.baytowntwpmn.govoffice2.com

See also Greater Stillwater Chamber of Commerce, p. 88.

See Stillwater and Hudson for lodging options.

BAYPORT TOUR

See map on p. 71.

Though Bayport has no National Register structures, the city does, for all its industrial inheritance, have a hidden side: Victorian-era houses of such size and beauty as to rival any of the historic neighborhoods of Hudson or Hastings. The community's diminutive size makes the viewing of such unexpected treasures a sheer delight.

Bayport's main thoroughfare divides the city neatly. On the east of the St. Croix Trail (Highway 95) lies the old industrial heart of Baytown. Though the historic railroad buildings are completely gone and the Andersen Corporation campus dominates the lakefront, one can still find remnants of industrial village life at the turn of the twentieth century.

Cross over to the western side of town and pass through a tiny business district with vestiges of the city as it might have looked before World War I, and you will be in the heart of the 1880s and 1890s town, with block after block of residential wonders. Historic cemeteries are there as well. And running downhill from the west neighborhoods into the east neighborhoods and through the parks, still in its controlled form, is Joe Perro's creek, which became the millrace for Ambrose Secrest's flouring mill.

As have Hastings, Afton, Stillwater, Marine on St. Croix, and Taylors Falls, Bayport will, in the near future, research the historic construction and ownership of its marvelous residential housing district, consider what merits National Register status, and begin the work of putting Bayport firmly in a place of honor among its sister cities on the St. Croix.

Note that Central Avenue is the north-south dividing line for both the numbered streets *and* avenues.

1. AVERY LOG CABIN RESORT (C. 1930)
333 Lake Street South

The last of the cabin resorts to be found in this vicinity. Marvelously eclectic architecture, likely by the owners.

2. OLD RAILROAD BOARDINGHOUSE (C. 1876)
Maine Street North at 1st Avenue North

Commissioned by Louis Torinus for working men at the St. Croix Lumber Company.

3. FIRST SETTLERS DEDICATION MARKER (1976)
Maine Street North at 1st Avenue North

The plaque marks the location of the first settlement in Bayport. François Bruce settled here in a blockhouse in 1842.

4. ANDERSEN LUMBER COMPANY OFFICES (C. 1915)
Maine Street North at 5th Avenue North

5. RESIDENCE
655 2nd Street North

6. CLASSIC BUNGALOWS (C. 1925)
251 and 295 4th Avenue North

7. WORKER'S COTTAGES (C. 1900)
247, 263, and 297 5th Avenue North (one cottage at rear)

8. ST. MICHAEL'S CEMETERY (1859)
6th Street North at 8th Avenue North

9. HAZELWOOD CEMETERY (1851)
5th Avenue North at 8th Street North

10. OLD LIVERY BARN (C. 1880)
507 6th Street North

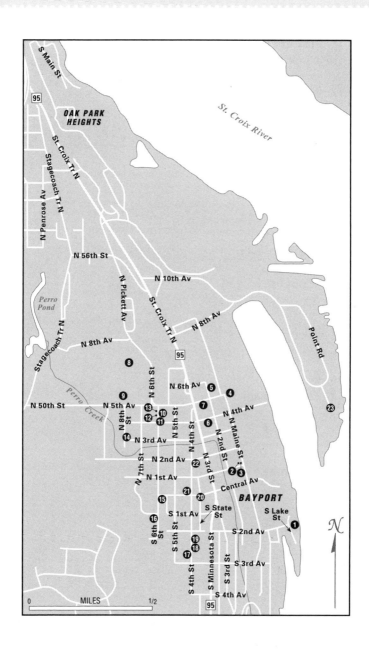

S Main St

95

OAK PARK
HEIGHTS

St. Croix River

St. Croix Tr N

Stagecoach Tr N

N Penrose Av

N 56th St

N 10th Av

Perro
Pond

N Pickett Av

St. Croix Tr N

N 8th Av

Point Rd

Stagecoach Tr N

N 8th Av

95

8

Perro Creek

N 6th St

N 6th Av

5

4

9

N 50th St

N 5th Av

13

7

23

N 8th St

12

10

N 5th St

11

6

N 4th Av

N Maine St

N 2nd St

14

N 3rd Av

22

N 4th St

N 3rd St

N 7th St

N 2nd Av

N 1st Av

21

20

Central Av

BAYPORT

15

S 1st Av

S State St

S 2nd Av

S Lake St

1

16

S 6th St

S 5th St

19

18

S Minnesota St

S 3rd St

S 3rd Av

N

17

S 4th St

S 4th Av

0   MILES   1/2

95

11. RESIDENCE
4th Avenue North at 6th Street North

12. RESIDENCE
594 6th Street North

13. RESIDENCE
528 6th Street North

14. RESIDENCE
8th Street North at 3rd Avenue North

15. RESIDENCE
128 6th Street South

16. RESIDENCE
212 6th Street South

17. RESIDENCE
347 4th Street South

18. RESIDENCE
380 4th Street South

19. RESIDENCE
355 2nd Avenue South

20. RESIDENCE
102 State Street South

21. RESIDENCE
114 4th Street North

22. RESIDENCE
297 4th Street North

23. KITTSON'S POINT

Norman Kittson's American Fur Company trading post was housed in a cabin out on this spit of land.

OAK PARK HEIGHTS

This tiny city, platted as Oak Park in 1857 by John Parker, has gone through more transformations than perhaps any community in the St. Croix Valley.

A longtime residential river village of ten blocks, with only very modest industry, it was placed firmly in the public mind when the new state penitentiary was built on its southern boundaries, bringing Oak Park jobs, notoriety, press, and new residents, all of which rose up around a community that still has lovely vestiges of its nineteenth-century roots.

The village, shaped as a long rectangle, had its eastern boundaries on the river frontage. Situated between Stillwater and Bayport (South Stillwater), it was little more than a pass-through for several government roads and, later, rail lines, coming and going between the two larger communities. A waiting platform for the St. Paul, Stillwater and Taylors Falls Railroad (later the Chicago, St. Paul, Minneapolis and Omaha Railroad) was placed at Oak Park Station, where present-day Stagecoach Trail once crossed the tracks at the northern end of the village.

David Cover, a riverboat pilot, was among the first to settle on the land in the 1840s, dealing in lumber. Parker relocated from Stillwater in 1850. Early development included a sawmill and a cooperage for making barrels, both on the riverfront. Business was centered on Mill Street, which in its time would have been found just where highways 36 and 95 (the northern terminus of Stagecoach Trail) now intersect.

The village, being adjacent to Stillwater, with high bluffs overlooking Lake St. Croix, drew some wealthy families to build substantial homes, and a large public park was also established. Settlers included transplanted New Englanders and immigrants from the United Kingdom, Germany, and Scandinavia.

Highway 36 was extended from Minneapolis out

Red Mill crew, Oak Park, 1904

to the St. Croix River in the 1930s, crossing through the village and bisecting it into north and south districts. And the Works Progress Administration's Civilian Conservation Corps (CCC) was also active in that time, working to beautify the burgeoning tourism area with handsome stonework road walls and overlooks. Though the new roadway enabled automobile tourist traffic to more easily reach the river villages, travelers mostly went north to Stillwater or south to Bayport and the lake villages. And each time the highway was improved (widened), a little more of historic Oak Park disappeared. Oak Park Heights Township was replatted and established in 1938 and incorporated as a city in 1959.

Highway 36, which bisected the remaining small nineteenth-century residential district on the north side of the highway and the older residential area known as "The Village" and the vast campus of the state penitentiary on the south side of the highway, offers a substantial number of lodging, eating, and shopping venues on the Minnesota side of the river.

A proposal for an extension of Highway 36 across Lake St. Croix to Hudson as a replacement for the aging historic lift bridge in Stillwater brought about wholesale clearances of Oak Park neighborhoods, sixty-six buildings in all, including many of the nineteenth-century bluff houses and most of the riverfront mill district. The bridge project stalled in the late 1990s, with reviews of environmental impact. Population pressures continue to push the concept of the new bridge as ever more Wisconsin residents commute daily to the Minneapolis–St. Paul metropolitan area.

Now much enlarged from its days as a platted village, Oak Park Heights might be considered a bedroom community of Stillwater, but it has become a significant district in its own right, supported not only by its extensive commercial offerings but also by the city's progressive planning for public parklands, nature preserves, and a system of trails on which to reach these carefully tended and well-managed natural areas. The city employs a full-time arborist, among its other civic appointments.

Contact the City of Oak Park Heights or the Greater Stillwater Chamber of Commerce for a park and trail guide.

 LOCAL RESOURCES

City of Oak Park Heights
651-439-4439
www.cityofoakparkheights.com

Boutwells Landing Museum
Boutwells Landing Senior Living Center
5600 Norwich Parkway
Oak Park Heights, MN 55082
651-439-5956
http://wchsmn.org/museums/boutwells_landing
www.boutwells.com
Open daily.

See also Greater Stillwater Chamber of Commerce, p. 88.

LODGING OPTIONS

Cover Park Manor Bed and Breakfast
15330 North 58th Street
Oak Park Heights, MN 55082
651-430-9292
coverpark@coverpark.com
www.coverpark.com

See also Hudson and Stillwater for lodging options.

OAK PARK HEIGHTS TOUR

See map on p. 77.

Oak Park Heights, having gone unrecognized for most of its existence as a historic district, suddenly found itself with three new National Register properties after a comprehensive cultural resource survey was completed to record the sixty-six residential and commercial buildings that were about to be lost to the new bridge proposed in the 1990s. The great campus of the state penitentiary had already been placed on the National Register in 1986.

In addition to the newly designated sites, Oak Park Heights shelters some lovely residential structures up the hillsides above the lake.

It is best to approach this district from the south. Leave Highway 95 above Bayport when you see the sign offering an alternate route into Stillwater. Pickett Avenue runs along the east boundaries of the Minnesota Correctional Facility and winds its way up to Stagecoach Trail. You are now on the old Point Douglas–Superior government road.

"NR" indicates National Register properties.

1. STATE PRISON HISTORIC DISTRICT/MINNESOTA CORRECTIONAL FACILITY (1910–1914, NR)
5500 Pickett Avenue

Administration building, Minnesota State Prison, Oak Park, 1926

This brick prison complex was built just before World War I, along with two warden's residences. The architect for the entire project was state architect Clarence Howard Johnston, Sr. Not open to the public.

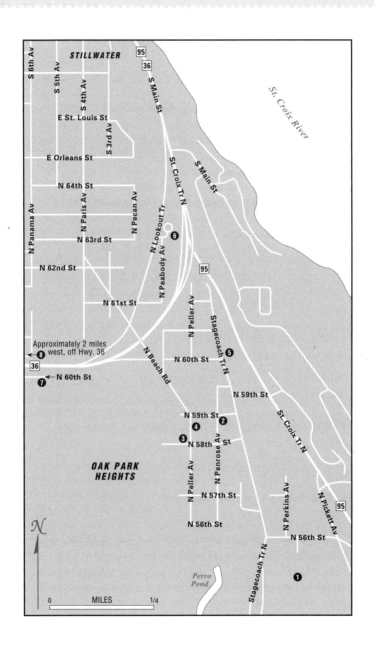

2. JOHN AND SUSAN (NÉE COVER) PARKER HOUSE (C. 1860s)
5870 Stagecoach Trail

3. DAVID COVER HOUSE/COVER PARK MANOR (C. 1880)
15330 North 58th Street

4. RESIDENCE
5855 Peller Avenue North

5. MORITZ BERGSTEIN SHODDY MILL AND WAREHOUSE (C. 1890, NR)
6046 Stagecoach Road

The Bergstein mill is all that remains of the once thriving commercial district of Oak Park. All other buildings were removed during the razing of structures for the proposed Stillwater-Houlton bridge in the 1990s.

6. STILLWATER OVERLOOK (1938, NR)
Lookout Trail near 63rd Street North

One of many CCC projects completed by the camp crew at Bayport.

7. THE LOG CABIN/PHIL'S TARA HIDEAWAY (1932, NR)
15021 60th Street North

An excellent example of postwar roadside architecture.

8. BOUTWELLS LANDING MUSEUM
5600 Norwich Parkway

Boutwells Landing Museum, with St. Croix artifacts, photographs, and exhibits and the old one-room Oak Park schoolhouse (1864), is under the care and guidance of the Washington County Historical Society. Free and open to the public.

STILLWATER AND STILLWATER TOWNSHIP

The earliest settlement on the site of present-day Stillwater was made by former trader, soldier, and justice of the peace Joseph Renshaw Brown, who, in 1838, built a mud and tamarack cabin near the outlet of the stream that would later bear his name. From this shack he set up fur-trading operations and platted a townsite he named Dahkotah (Dacotah, Dakotah), at the head of Lake St. Croix. Brown began building a courthouse and a jail and encouraging settlement when Dahkotah became the seat of St. Croix County, Wisconsin Territory, which, at that time, looped in the western shore of Lake St. Croix.

The Lake House for laborers was built in 1840. Anson Northrup built the first hotel in Washington County in 1841. Sylvester Stateler was the town's first blacksmith (1842), and the first steamboat, the *Otter,* landed at Dahkotah in 1843, carrying mill equipment. The town was renamed Still Water in 1843 by John McKusick, one of countless Maine lumbermen who had made their way west. Jacob Fisher sold his claim just below Dahkotah for the building of the first lumber mill on the lake, the Stillwater Lumber Company, which began operations in 1844.

By 1846, Stillwater had ten families and some two dozen single men; a post office was established in 1846. Dahkotah, where Brown's courthouse had never been completed, was abandoned, and Stillwater was made the new St. Croix County seat. The town and the post office were transferred to the Minnesota Territory in 1849, where the community retained its status as a county seat, now of Washington County.

A fine new county courthouse of wood was built in 1849 at the top of Chestnut Street. Also in 1849 the decision was made to establish the territorial prison at Stillwater. The massive structure was eventually sited in a deep ravine atop a historic 1839 Ojibwe-Dakota battle site known locally as Battle Hollow.

Stillwater expanded rapidly as a lumber mill town in the 1850s. With the rivers connecting to the northern pinelands, quiet water to assemble great log rafts (the boom site), and waterpower to run the mills, Stillwater became the preeminent site for steam-powered lumber mills. A log boom was built just north of the town, and soon, with the early stage routes connecting the city to St. Paul, Marine, and Point Douglas, Stillwater became the center of all things lumber.

Isaac Staples, who had been making heavy investments in pinelands to the north and had considerable logging operations in place (with and without government permission), decided to settle permanently in Stillwater and erect a sawmill in 1853 on the lower shore of the town.

St. Croix Boom Company site, two miles north of Stillwater, 1898

Isaac Staples's St. Croix steam lumber mill, Stillwater, c1875

Stillwater was incorporated in 1854, with McKusick elected as mayor. A handsome brick armory was built in Stillwater in 1855, and a new business structure, the Sawyer Block, was erected in 1856 as the first stone building in the city. Sawyer and Heaton had opened a lumber mill that was proving very successful. Other mills followed along the shores of Stillwater, Oak Park, and South Stillwater, including the McKusick, Andersen and Company, the St. Croix Lumber Company, the Hersey Lumber Company, and the Turnbull mill. The Sawyer House Hotel (a sawyer is a skilled lumberman) became the leading hostelry, catering to a very different kind of tenant and becoming a popular site for the social elite and for area conventions.

In the years before the Civil War, most residents were wealthy lumber or rail barons; middle-class professionals such as lawyers, physicians, and merchants; or laborers working in the mills, on the docks, on the railroads, and on the log booms or plying modest trades such as farrier, blacksmith, laundress, leatherworker, housemaid, barber, hotel kitchen worker, shoemaker, or saloonkeeper. The city established the necessary civic services: a fire department with a hook and ladder division, a police department, a guard (militia), several savings banks, a water company, a gaslight company, and a telegraph office.

By 1860, Stillwater could boast three saloons in every block downtown. The town was now crowded with workers' hotels and boardinghouses—Stillwater House, Minnesota House, Lake House, and Liberty House, among others—where a bed (often shared by three) and a communal meal in the large dining rooms provided a gathering place for men of many nationalities to talk, joke, swap stories, improve their English, and get news from the homeland.

The first non-Yankees had been arriving for a decade from Scandinavia, Ireland, and Italy, and more came every week on the boats moving upriver or migrated down from Canada looking for work in the pineries, on the booms, and in the mills. Mail—and new immigrants—saw daily delivery to Stillwater by steamboat and by rail. At week's end, with pay in their pockets, the workingmen of the city moved on to the saloons and billiard halls for the night, waking up heavy headed and with emptied pockets on Saturday morning. On Sunday morning they went to church.

President Lincoln's April 1861 call for 75,000 volunteers to answer the South's secession prompted Washington County to fill out companies in seven volunteer regiments, with Company B of the First Minnesota Regiment almost entirely composed of the men of the Stillwater Guards. Company D of the Third Minnesota was almost fully made up of Scandinavians—seventy Swedes and thirty Norwegians. Company K of the Fifth Minnesota was very nearly all Irish.

Of these regiments, the First Minnesota was most often in harm's way, being at Bull Run and the Peninsula Campaign and most notably at Gettysburg, in defense of Little Round Top, where the First covered itself with glory, though not without great loss. In the succeeding years of the war, more recruits were called up, and Washington County sent hundreds more men. Captain John Oliver, who had settled at Lakeland, supplied six sons. Ninety-eight men alone came from Taylors Falls, Afton, Lakeland, and Stillwater, with a large roster of Swedes from the lumber camps. And in 1862, the U.S.–Dakota War broke out along the Minnesota River, and recruits of the Third, Sixth, and Seventh Minnesota regiments were sent to Fort Ridgely. The conflict began when a small group of Dakota warriors attacked white settlers in response to late annuity payments and the ensuing starvation this caused. The fighting lasted six weeks, and many on both sides were killed. In the end, thousands of Dakota were interned at Fort Snelling and then forced to leave Minnesota.

AFTER THE CIVIL WAR

With the end of the war and mustering out of companies, Washington County's men began returning home, walking, wounded, or in pine boxes shipped north by train for burial. Committees were formed in all villages and towns to consider how best to commemorate the fallen. The year 1865 was one of quiet stocktaking. Fairview Cemetery was organized in 1867 in South Stillwater, and all bodies buried in the district's cemetery of 1846 were moved to the new burial ground.

Sawyer House, Stillwater, 1870

Within a few years life was back on track in every sense. Housing flourished in Stillwater, and money could be made in every trade, skill, and profession. More hotels were built, and more boardinghouses, more cottages, and many more grand and expensive residences were raised atop the hills and bluffs

Looking southwest along Main Street from Chestnut, Stillwater, 1878

overlooking the city. The city's business district seemed to be under constant construction as additional brick commercial structures and blocks were built for offices and workrooms. Gas lighting was installed throughout the business district in 1875, with electric lights following by 1888.

The first county courthouse, then twenty-five years old, was replaced with a grand new stone and brick structure designed by the architect Augustus Knight in 1869 atop Zion Hill. Overlooking all of Stillwater and Lake St. Croix, the historic Washington County Courthouse would serve for over a century.

An opera house, the largest west of Chicago, was built on the site of the old Minnesota House Hotel on Main Street in 1881. The Sawyer House hosted elegant social events attended by Stillwater's wealthy and elite. Veterans of the Civil War held their reunions and banquets there, establishing the famous tontine the Last Man's Club in the 1880s.

A telephone service line was run out to Stillwater from St. Paul in 1880, with a branch north to Marine. A charter from the legislature permitted an engine-driven drawbridge to be built across Lake St. Croix to Houlton, Wisconsin, in 1875. Flouring mills joined the lumber

mills all around Stillwater. Even the lumber baron Isaac
Staples took a hand at grain milling, building the St.
Croix Flour Mill in 1877 on the north end of town.
Foundries, machine shops, furniture factories, sash and
blind factories, carriage and wagon shops, boat factories,
blacksmiths, and livery stables flourished. Providers of
provender—bakers, meat cutters, fruit and vegetable
vendors, milk and cheese companies, and six breweries—
now labored to serve the city's growing population.

Steamboat traffic reached its peak in the 1880s and
1890s, with the city levee usually crowded with boat
traffic of every description. Local firms offered shipping,
tug service, local transport, and tourist excursions up the
St. Croix and down the Mississippi River. This coincided
with the arrival of the streetcar and more rail lines, a
quiet but insistent signal that river transport would
begin to lose out to overland transportation services.

STILLWATER AFTER 1900

By the turn of the century, the pineries were thinned out
and the lumber mills were closing. The last lumber rafts
left Lake St. Croix in 1914, the same year that Stillwater's largest manufacturer, the Minnesota Thresher Company, failed and one of Stillwater's largest structures,
the territorial prison, was closed as all staff and inmates
moved south to the new state prison built at Oak Park.
The levee was rehabilitated as a handsome city park,
doing away with much of the old mill structures, warehouses, docks, and machinery that had once embodied
the city's most important industries.

The population, which had reached a high of
13,000 in the 1880s, began to decline at the same time
and continued to do so through World War I. Some
Stillwater businesses rallied to stay even with the times,
and the government boats the *Minnesota, Iowa, Illinois,*
and *Missouri* were built at Stillwater in 1921 for service
on the lower rivers, indicating the continuation of at

Steamers at the Stillwater levee, 1902

least one of the city's claims to fame. But it was not to last. The Twin City Forge and Foundry, which had survived the war years, failed on the eve of the Depression in 1930, and the Omaha Railroad took out its tracks in 1935. The rise of the automobile, the development of state parks, the creation of good roads, and tourism promotion helped stabilize Stillwater after World War II.

Expanding from town, Stillwater Township comprises several suburbs and more rural villages on the city's northern outskirts. Highway 36, which had undergone considerable improvements in the 1930s, now boasted businesses on both sides coming into Stillwater. And the spectacular new Stillwater Lift Bridge, the last of its kind in this region, had been built across Lake St. Croix to Houlton in 1931, replacing the old swing bridge to accommodate the new automobile and truck traffic for the city.

But of greatest importance to history-minded travelers was Minnesota's rediscovery of its treasure of Lake St. Croix and Stillwater's investment in rehabilitating its magnificent architectural heritage. The great houses on the hills were refurbished into the Victorian painted

Old Stillwater-Houlton bridge, May 1930

ladies they once were, becoming homes again to the wealthy and famous or repurposed as popular bed-and-breakfast establishments for the increasing number of eager visitors to the city's historic sites.

There have been some losses. Many old waterfront buildings have been demolished. The ravine that was famous as Battle Hollow and, later, as the site of Minnesota's first territorial prison has been filled with contemporary housing. Some historic residential structures are in danger of being torn down for property redevelopment owing to their lack of local or National Register status protection.

But a great many other buildings and houses have been restored or protected and put to new use. The entire Main Street business district received National Register protection and has attracted promising commercial tenants and the attention of other historic towns in the state that saw what could be possible in the restoration of the heart of a city with so many wonderful stories to tell.

ⓘ LOCAL RESOURCES

City of Stillwater
216 North 4th Street
Stillwater, MN 55082
651-430-8800
www.ci.stillwater.mn.us
Website has excellent neighborhood histories under "Community Information."

Greater Stillwater Chamber of Commerce
Heartland Office Village
1950 Northwestern Avenue
Suite 101
Stillwater, MN 55082
651-439-4001
info@ilovestillwater.com
www.ilovestillwater.com
www.discoverstillwater.com

Stillwater Traveler
www.stillwatertraveler.com

Washington County Historic Courthouse
101 West Pine Street
Stillwater, MN 55082
651-275-7075
www.co.washington.mn.us/hc
Open Monday thru Friday, 8:00 a.m. to 4:00 p.m.

Arcola Mills Historic Foundation
12905 Arcola Trail North
PO Box 247 (mailing address)
Stillwater, MN 55082
651-439-1652
info@arcolamills.org
www.arcolamills.org

🛏 LODGING OPTIONS

The Stillwater Bed and Breakfast Association
651-351-1187
www.stillwateratoz.com

See also Hudson for lodging options.

STILLWATER TOUR

See map on p. 91.

Given its ninety-one National Register properties, it would not be far from the truth to say that the entire city of Stillwater is one huge historic district. Of those ninety-one structures and sites, seventy-seven are contained in the Stillwater Commercial Historic District. The tour map outlines the boundaries of this district and highlights some special structures. This is walking tour time, particularly since many of the streets and alleys are narrow and traffic is constant. Parking your car in one of the city lots a block above the main street will give you the time and freedom to wander (and, inevitably, shop).

You can also enjoy the quiet streets and shady lanes of the upper residential neighborhoods. Here are the houses of the great and the near great of the nineteenth century and the smaller but lovely houses of the post–Civil War professional middle class of Stillwater society. An extraordinary range of architectural styles is displayed, and you will find touring by car a relaxing experience. There are some nonresidential treasures on Stillwater's heights: church row, handsome schools, a historic city cemetery, and, of course, the jewel of the city, the Washington County Courthouse.

For a full listing of National Register properties in Stillwater and Stillwater Township, see the Minnesota National Register of Historic Places Database, http://nrhp.mnhs.org/nrsearch.cfm.

When driving into town, take the Osgood/4th Street exit from Highway 36, and drive north into Stillwater to Marsh Street. Then, go right one block, and come into Stillwater via 3rd Street. This way, you will avoid all the backed-up traffic traveling through Stillwater on the main street and be able to stop and walk through Fairview Cemetery on the way. Continuing on 3rd Street, you will pass the historic county courthouse. You can tour the residential neighborhoods by car on these upper heights and then make your way down to the public parking lots on 2nd Street, one block up the hill from Main Street. And unless you are willing to wait a long time for the pleasure of crossing the historic lift bridge, admire it from below in the equally historic (and much older) Lowell Park.

"NR" indicates National Register properties.

1. HISTORIC FAIRVIEW CEMETERY (1867), SALEM GERMAN EVANGELICAL LUTHERAN CEMETERY (1880s)
North Osgood Avenue/South 4th Street at Orleans Street

Fairview is a forty-acre nondenominational burial ground and the site of a statue of Sam Bloomer, color bearer for the First Minnesota Regiment in the Civil War. Salem Cemetery is immediately adjacent to Fairview. Both are open sunup to sundown.

2. ALBERT LAMMERS HOUSE (1893, NR)
1306 South 3rd Street

An elaborate Queen Anne frame residence built in 1893.

3. RESIDENCE (1890s)
1304 South 3rd Street

Built in the Neoclassical style promoted by the Great Exposition in Chicago, 1892.

4. NELSON SCHOOL (1897, NR)
1018 South 1st Street

Built in the Georgian/Classical Revival style designed by Orff and Guilbert.

South Hill Residential District

5. HISTORIC WASHINGTON COUNTY COURTHOUSE (1870, NR)
100 West Pine Street

The state's oldest standing courthouse is now open to the public as a museum, archive, education center, and

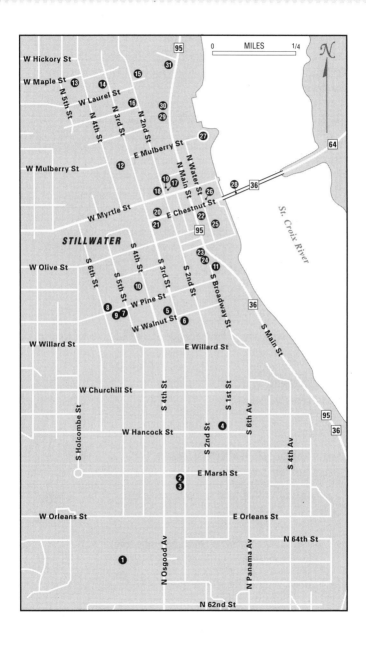

W Hickory St

W Maple St

W Laurel St

W Mulberry St

E Mulberry St

STILLWATER

W Myrtle St

E Chestnut St

W Olive St

W Pine St

W Walnut St

W Willard St

E Willard St

W Churchill St

W Hancock St

E Marsh St

W Orleans St

E Orleans St

N 64th St

N 62nd St

N 5th St

N 4th St

N 3rd St

N 2nd St

N Main St

N Water St

S 6th St

S 5th St

S 4th St

S 3rd St

S 2nd St

S Broadway St

S Main St

S Holcombe St

S 4th St

S 1st St

S 2nd St

S 6th Av

S 4th Av

N Osgood Av

N Panama Av

St. Croix River

MILES   0   1/4

N

95   31   15   30   29   27   16   12   13   14   19   17   18   26   28   36   20   22   25   21   23   24   11   95   10   8   9   7   5   6   4   2   3   1   64   36   95

site for special events including lectures, concerts, receptions, and Civil War reenactments. There is a Civil War monument and plaque on the grounds. Open weekdays or by appointment.

6. ST. MICHAEL'S CATHOLIC CHURCH (1872)
611 South 3rd Street

Built in the French Second Empire style.

7. AUSTIN JENKS HOUSE (1871, NR)
504 South 5th Street

A Victorian brick residence built for Captain Jenks, a river pilot and ship owner who was involved in log rafting.

8. RESIDENCE (1880)
320 West Pine Street

A Shingle style three-story residence in the New England style.

9. RESIDENCE (C. 1870)
305 West Pine Street

French Second Empire frame residence.

10. ROSCOE HERSEY HOUSE (1879, NR)
416 South 4th Street

An Eastlake/Queen Anne residence designed by George Orff.

11. MORTIMER WEBSTER HOUSE (1866, NR)
435 South Broadway

An Italian Villa–style frame residence.

12. STILLWATER PUBLIC LIBRARY (1902; RENOVATION 1987)

224 North 3rd Street

The strong brick design of the original Carnegie library can still be viewed in the midst of an exceptionally sensitive and handsome renovation.

North Hill Residential District

13. WILLIAM SAUNTRY HOUSE AND RECREATION HALL (1901–2, NR)

626 North 4th Street and 625 North 5th Street

A large Queen Anne frame residence and whimsical Exotic Revival recreation facility.

14. RESIDENCE (C. 1890)

614 North 3rd Street

Built in the late-nineteenth-century "modern" Craftsman style.

15. MURDOCK HOUSE (1859)

210 East Laurel Street

A Greek Revival and Italianate design, currently the Laurel Street B&B. Tours by appointment: 651-351-0031.

16. IVORY MCKUSICK HOUSE (1868, NR)

504 North 2nd Street

A small French Second Empire frame residence.

17. STILLWATER POST OFFICE (1903)

220 East Myrtle Street

This former post office was built in the Classic Revival style.

Stillwater Commercial Historic District

18. THE LOWELL INN (1927, NR)
102 North 2nd Street

The Lowell Inn is as famous for its restaurant as it is for its elegant lodging. Built on the site of the old Sawyer House and named for that society hotel's last proprietor, Elmore Lowell.

19. H. C. FARMER SUNKEN GARDEN AND FOUNTAIN (1935, NR)
113 North 2nd Street

20. PENNY/BRUNSWICK HOUSE (C. 1848)
114 East Chestnut

Believed to be the oldest residence still standing in Stillwater. Now listed as a "contributing property" in the Historic District, at risk for demolition.

21. STILLWATER ARMORY (1922, NR)
107 East Chestnut Street

22. BRINE'S RESTAURANT (1860, NR)
219 South Main Street

23. PACIFIC HOTEL (1872, NR)
402 South Main Street

24. JOSEPH WOLF BREWERY BUILDING, OFFICE, AND TUNNEL/CAVE SYSTEM (1872, NR)
412 to 520 Main Street

Joseph Wolf Brewery Cave Tours are offered on weekends and by appointment. Call Luna Rossa Café at 651-430-0560.

Wolf's Brewery and the Lowell Band, Stillwater, July 4, 1912

25. CHICAGO, MILWAUKEE AND ST. PAUL RAILROAD FREIGHT DEPOT/FREIGHTHOUSE RESTAURANT (1883, NR)
305 South Water Street

26. LUMBERMEN'S EXCHANGE BUILDING/WATER STREET INN (1890, NR)
101 South Water Street

27. LOWELL PARK AND PAVILION (1916, NR)
Foot of Mulberry Street

Leaving Central Stillwater

28. STILLWATER LIFT BRIDGE (1931, NR)
Foot of Chestnut Street

This eighty-year-old ten-span concrete and metal vertical-lift highway bridge is one of only three remaining in the region.

29. ISAAC STAPLES SAWMILL/STAPLES MILL ANTIQUES MALL
410 North Main Street

30. STAPLES MILL/ST. CROIX LUMBER MILLS POWERHOUSE (1850, NR)
318 North Main Street

31. TERRITORIAL PRISON SITE (1849, 1884) AND WARDEN'S HOUSE (1853, NR)
602 North Main Street

The last buildings of the old territorial prison built in Battle Hollow burned down in 2005, but the warden's house remains and is the home of the Washington County Historical Society and the Warden's House Museum.

Minnesota State Prison and warden's house, Stillwater, 1885

STILLWATER TOWNSHIP AND ARCOLA MILLS TOUR

The village of Arcola was platted in 1846 and was the third site on the St. Croix where sawmills were built. The Arcola Mill was erected in 1846 by Martin Mower and partners on land at the north end of what had been dubbed the Buck Horn Prairie. The lumbering industry was very profitable, and Martin Mower and his brother John built a handsome Greek Revival house. Soon Arcola could also boast a general store run by John, carpentry and blacksmithing shops, a small boat-building enterprise, and some small houses built by the Mowers for their millhands, all situated around the Mower mansion.

After the Civil War years, Martin Mower was eventually able to wrest control of the St. Croix Boom Company from Isaac Staples in the 1880s and had a hand in most river traffic up and down the St. Croix. John Mower would become a representative to the fifth and sixth legislatures for three counties—Washington, Chisago, and Pine—and would return one more time for the seventeenth. Mower County in Minnesota is named for him.

Mower residence, Arcola Mills, c1900

He died at Arcola in 1879. Martin Mower never incorporated Arcola. He died at Arcola in 1890, and the mill closed down. Neither of the brothers had ever married.

Though Arcola was rewarded in 1911 with a passenger and freight station for the Minneapolis, St. Paul and Sault Ste. Marie Railroad when the great high bridge was built, by 1920 Arcola had become a ghost town.

Dr. Henry Van Meier and his wife, Katherine, purchased the residence and the entire fifty acres surrounding the house during the Depression for a summer home, collecting nine small buildings from around the St. Croix district and installing them for use by friends and family, students and scholars, and writers and artists to take a retreat for a week or a month during the summer. The importance of the house itself brought historic preservation attention to the Mower/Van Meier house in the late 1970s, and the house, barn, and remaining mill chimney were put on the National Register in 1980 before the death of Dr. Van Meier. Katherine Van Meier established a foundation to ensure the continuation of their tradition of an eclectic summer arts community.

Stillwater Township

1. DUTCHTOWN ADDITION, STILLWATER (1853–1902)
Highway 95 immediately south of intersection with Highway 96

A company mill town built a mile north of Stillwater by the Schulenberg and Boeckler Lumber Company, originally named Charlottenburg by its German population.

2. STONE BRIDGE (1863, NR) AND BROWNS CREEK
Country Road 5 (Stonebridge Trail North) south of Highway 96 at Brown's Creek

A stone arch bridge of locally quarried limestone built to span Brown's Creek on the Point Douglas–Superior government road.

3. RUTHERFORD PIONEER CEMETERY (1850s)

Take Highway 96 west to Manning Avenue (County Road 15), and turn south to Rutherford Cemetery.

4. BOUTWELL PIONEER CEMETERY (1850s)
Minar Avenue at 80th Street

5. HENRY STUSSI HOUSE (1878, NR)
9097 Mendel Road north of Highway 96

A Victorian Gothic brick residence using a plan from Palliser and Palliser's *American Cottage Homes.*

6. WASHINGTON COUNTY POOR FARM AND CEMETERY (1858, 1924) AND OUTING LODGE AT PINE POINT
11661 Myeron Road (County Road 61)

A plat of land was purchased by the county in 1858 to be utilized as a place of residence and farming for the county's needy. The mansion and parklands have been fully restored as an award-winning lodge and conference center. Open for tours. Call 651-439–9747 or see www.outinglodge.com.

7. PEST HOUSE (1872, NR)
9033 Fairy Falls Road (County Road 11)

This large wood residential structure was built by the Washington County Board of Health after the Civil War as the county's pest house, a clinic and sanatorium for persons inflicted with nineteenth-century contagious diseases such as smallpox, scarlet fever, typhoid, and diphtheria. The house has been privately owned and re-furbished as a residence since 1910.

8. ST. CROIX BOOM SITE (1856–1914, NR AND NATIONAL HISTORIC LANDMARK)
Highway 95, three miles north of Stillwater (currently closed)

The St. Croix boom site, sitting at the top of Lake St. Croix, was the final destination for the great log drives down from the northern pineries via the tributaries into the St. Croix River. Logs would be stored, sorted by brand marks for ownership, maneuvered into rafts, and tied together to send down the lake to the lumber mills. The boom company collected a fee of forty cents per thousand board feet delivered.

A wayside rest and parking area on the bluff above the boom site were built in the 1930s during the CCC era. MnDOT has closed the wayside rest and parking areas as a result of budget cuts, and access remains limited. The boom site is now on the watch list with the National Historic Landmarks program.

9. ST. CROIX BOOM COMPANY SUPERINTENDENT'S HOUSE AND BARN (1855, NR)
Highway 95 (North St. Croix Trail)

A Queen Ann–style frame residence built for the St. Croix Boom Company superintendent W. F. McGray. Privately owned; not open to the public.

Logs being sorted for rafting, St. Croix boom site, 1907

Arcola Mills

10. SOO LINE HIGH BRIDGE (1911, NR)
Arcola Trail North

Bridge design experts have called the Soo Line High (or Arcola) Bridge the most spectacular multispan steel arch bridge in the world. C. A. P. ("Cap") Turner's spectacular steel deck railroad bridge soars to 184 feet above Lake St. Croix, anchored on the high bluffs of Wisconsin and Minnesota.

11. MOWER HOUSE AND ARCOLA MILL SITE (1980, NR)
12905 Arcola Trail North

Take Highway 95 north from the intersection with Highway 96, and then take the first right-hand turn-off. This is Arcola Trail North. Drive to the north end of the Arcola Trail, about three miles; watch for the Arcola Mills gate and sign. (If you reach Highway 95 again, you have just passed the site.) The Mower house is known as the third-oldest and the largest timber-frame house in the state and sits amid one of the largest undisturbed parcels of land on the St. Croix River. The house and grounds have been undergoing continued renovation and are open to the public for programs, workshops, and events.

MARINE DISTRICT

MARINE ON ST. CROIX

Before Marine became Marine, the St. Croix Lumber Company was formed in the winter of 1837, and men, machinery, and supplies were sent upriver from St. Louis by the steamer *Palmyra*—the first on the St. Croix. Though the mill was never built, one of the party, L. W. Stratton, took the opportunity to stake a claim in December 1838, the first in what would later be Marine.

Originally called Judd's Mills, the name was changed to Marine Mill to reflect the town of Marine, Illinois, which was the home base of the many partners in the enterprise. It became the first commercial sawmill to be built on the banks of the St. Croix River.

Among the partners who traveled from Illinois was Orange Walker, a tanner from Vermont who would remain with the Marine Lumber Company for nearly half a century and manage the first mercantile establishment on the St. Croix that was not a trading post. Others who would become well known in their time

Walker, Judd, and Veazie sawmill and crew, Marine Mills, 1874

were Asa and Madison Parker, Dr. Lucius Green, Joseph Cottrell, William Dibble, Lewis Judd's brothers Samuel and George, Hiram Berkey and Samuel Berkleo, and the blacksmith Joseph McElroy. Orange Walker and George Judd later became sole owners.

In 1850, the lumber company was renamed Judd, Walker and Co. The town was platted as Marine Mills in 1853, the same year that the first stagecoaches began making their way to the village and that a schoolhouse was built. By this time the town offered a hotel—the Marine House—a brewery, a café, a blacksmith shop, a company store for millhands run by the Marine Mill, and a general store for the town community.

Most of the early settlers of the township were transplanted New Englanders. They were joined in the 1840s and 1850s by Scandinavian immigrants, most from Sweden, and a good sprinkling of Irish, German, Canadian, and English pioneers. During the winters many of the Swedes went to work in the pineries and the lumber camps; come planting season, they returned to their farms to put in wheat and rye.

Marine began producing enough grain to attract Dr. James Gaskill, who came to build a flour mill in 1855. A year later, the Marine Ferry was established to enable frequent passage across the river. The ferry, which would operate for a hundred years, was the only means of crossing the river between Stillwater, Minnesota, and Osceola, Wisconsin.

By the start of the Civil War, many of the mill partners had grown wealthy, and other equally prosperous settlers came to Marine Mills to make their contribution to town life and to build a fine house. The firm Walker, Judd, and Veazie had purchased a steamboat, the *G. B. Knapp*, which made daily runs between Marine Mills and Prescott. They also ran a stagecoach between Marine Mills and Stillwater and, in 1879, installed a telephone connection with Stillwater.

The Oakland Cemetery was organized as a nondenominational public burial ground in 1872. A village charter was drafted for incorporation in 1875. At the height of the lumber industry, in the 1880s, Marine Mills had many famous guests pass through. John Jacob Astor IV and Ulysses S. Grant both signed the register of the Marine House.

The Soo Line Railroad was extended through the village in 1887, bringing a swift end to the stagecoach line, which had normally carried not only daily passengers but also daily mail deliveries. Now the railroad promised year-round transportation, especially important in the winter when the river ice had frozen and the steamers could not reach the levees.

Then, suddenly, lumbering—and the fate of Marine Mills—moved into uncertain times. In just a few years, Walker, Judd, and Veazie were in bankruptcy, the buildings abandoned and the millhands and lumbermen left without work. The sawmill was torn down in the 1890s, and Marine Mills was no longer a lumber town. The Gaskill flouring mill continued on its steady course, the need for grinding grain constant in rural life. Life went on, but the little town faded steadily as the new century came in. By 1905, the population had dropped to

Glen below mill pond, Marine Mills, c1890

just over 750 residents, exactly half the figure of thirty years before.

With both lumber mills gone and tourism rising as an important source of income, in 1917 the Marine Mills community voted to change the town name to Marine on St. Croix. In the years that followed, some of the river's most beautiful summer estates were built near Marine. The automobile and greatly improved roads began the steady stream of summer visitors from St. Paul and Minneapolis. Marine began to take on a reputation as an idyllic summer colony.

World War II drew many into the service and the small communities up and down the river valley into active support for the war effort. At the war's end, a special gift came to the St. Croix Valley: Alice O'Brien, the daughter of logger William O'Brien of Marine Mills and Florida, gave the State of Minnesota 180 acres for a new state park to be named for her father. It would be the first Minnesota state park that was easily accessible from the Twin Cities.

The Marine ferry was still in operation and very busy in 1948, with ferryman George Mills tallying 3,500 cars across the river in that summer. In 1951, the widening and rerouting of north-south Highway 95 caused many historic buildings to be demolished.

The year 1952 was kinder. The new William O'Brien State Park was officially opened by the Minnesota Department of Conservation, and though the Marine Ferry discontinued operation at the end of the summer, George Mills immediately opened a boat and canoe rental service with great success.

In 1957, the Amherst Wilder Foundation purchased two square miles of land near Marine on St. Croix, to be known as the Wilder Forest, with the Science Museum of Minnesota cooperating in building the Wilder Nature Center as a year-round education and conference site.

In December 1969, a resident committee opted to buy the historic Marine Mill site for future preservation. That same year, the Science Museum of Minnesota sold the Wilder Nature Center to the Lee and Rose Warner Foundation; the education facility is now known as the Warner Nature Center.

In 1972, President Richard Nixon signed a bill that decreed the preservation of the lower St. Croix River, from Prescott up to Taylors Falls, as a scenic riverway, thus joining the lower river with the upper river as a wild and scenic riverway. The year 1973 saw the doubling of William O'Brien State Park's acreage through acquisition of large adjacent pioneer farms.

John Hackett of the Minnesota Historical Society began a survey of Marine on St. Croix as he prepared to submit a request for National Register District status for the entire village. Designation was approved in June 1974: the new historic district included sixty structures and one ruin.

Today visitors arrive by car and tour bus, bicycle and motorcycle, and also by train. The Osceola and St. Croix Railway runs a 1.5-hour excursion train that leaves the historic Soo Line depot in Osceola, Wisconsin, travels along the sandstone bluffs above the river, and then crosses over the St. Croix on the Cedar Bend Draw Bridge to the Minnesota side, passing through Copas and William O'Brien State Park and pulling in to Marine on St. Croix.

COPAS AND OTISVILLE

These tiny unincorporated communities still exist in the few buildings left from the days of rail service and busier times.

John Columbus, an Italian-Swiss immigrant and trader, had platted a town along the bluffs of the St. Croix River a few miles north of Marine Mills in the mid-1840s with Benjamin Otis, a hunter-trapper, and his Ojibwe wife, Mary. Copas christened it Otisville in honor of his friend and partner. Columbus also established a small log cabin store at this site on the St. Croix

River in 1854 with a partner from his own home village in the Italian Alps, John Copas. A steam mill was built there in 1857.

Francis Register, a clerk with the Marine Lumber Company, became a land agent and organized Vasa nearby in 1858, hoping to attract trade and settlement away from Marine Mills by naming the town for the sixteenth-century king of Sweden, Gustavus Vasa, as an enticement to Swedes. He paid Benjamin Otis and John Columbus to release the three hundred acres of Otisville land. Register placed the platted lots on the market at Christmas 1856 and by February had sold sixty-one. Register invested in a newspaper advertisement extolling Vasa's strong qualities.

John Columbus moved down to Stillwater and opened a mercantile store, but John Copas stayed on at Vasa and married a Swedish girl named Caroline Peterson. The little town, strung out for a good length north to south along the river, had already grown enough for a second store, a school, a three-story hotel called the Vasa House, a post office with Register as postmaster, and a saloon.

But the depression of 1857 caused all, including the mill, to fail. The little town faded, and the south section of Vasa was annexed by Marine Mills in late 1860, leaving the north end of the village to be renamed Otis by county commissioners. When Copas's old partner, John Columbus, died, Copas kept his promise to his friend and had him buried along with the body of his favorite dog at the far edge of the Copas farm.

The Soo Line came through in 1886, and a depot was put in at the northern end of the former Vasa site, restoring the town to the map with the construction of railroad freight buildings. John Copas died in 1911, and the Soo Line changed the depot name to honor the Civil War veteran. The Copas station shipped out over 100,000 bushels of potatoes yearly in the 1880s.

When trucking began to overtake the railroads, business faded at the Copas station, and eventually both freight and passenger service came to an end. The Copas depot was removed in 1963, and the last of the freight warehouses was taken down. Today, only two buildings remain at Copas: a small store that endures as the popular Crabtree's Kitchen and the schoolhouse, which has been used for years as an antiques and gift shop.

B. T. Otis's son Henry, a métis (half Ojibwe, half French Canadian) who had moved to Marine after the Civil War, went to the north end of Otisville, where his father and mother had first settled with John Columbus back in the 1840s, and built a log cabin down on the flats below the old platted town. The site became known as Log House Landing and was a gathering place for lumbermen and river travelers for many years. The large island in the midst of the river was named for the Otis family. By the late 1880s, Log House Landing had become such a popular landing place for steamboats that Otis gave the cabin over to a friend, Judge Nathaway (likely of the Nathaway tribe of northwestern Wisconsin), and built a new cabin out on the island to have a more peaceful life. He remained there until his death in 1937 at the age of ninety-three and was buried in Oakland Cemetery in Marine on St. Croix.

ⓘ LOCAL RESOURCES

City of Marine on St. Croix
121 Judd Street
Marine on St. Croix, MN 55047
651-433-3636
mosc@wdemail.com
http://marine.govoffice.com
Open Monday thru Thursday, 8:00 a.m. to 4:30 p.m.

Stonehouse Museum
241 5th Street
Marine on St. Croix, MN 55047
651-433-3636
Free and open Memorial Day thru Labor Day, Saturday and Sunday, 2:00 to 5:00 p.m., or by appointment, 651-433-5675.

continues

Marine Mill
Judd Street
Marine on St. Croix, MN 55047
507-697-6321 (MHS Site Management Office)
marinemill@mnhs.org
www.mnhs.org/marinemill
Free and open May thru October, dawn to dusk.

William O'Brien State Park
16821 O'Brien Trail North
Marine on St. Croix, MN 55047
651-433-0500
www.dnr.state.mn.us/state_parks/william_obrien

Dunrovin Retreat Center
15525 St. Croix Trail North
Marine on St. Croix, MN 55047
651-433-2486
dunrovin@dunrovin.org
www.dunrovin.org

St. Croix Watershed Research Station
16910 152nd Street North
Marine on St. Croix, MN 55047
651-433-5953
www.smm.org/scwrs

Lee and Rose Warner Nature Center
15375 Norell Avenue North
Marine on St. Croix, MN 55047
651-433-2427 ext. 10
wnc@smm.org
www.smm.org/warnernaturecenter
Trailside Museum is open to the public Monday thru Friday,
8:00 a.m. to 4:00 p.m.

Hay Lake School and Erickson Log House Museum
14020 195th Street North
Marine on St. Croix, MN 55047
651-433-4014
information@wchsmn.org
www.wchsmn.org/museums/scandia
Open Friday, Saturday, and Sunday, 1:00 to 4:00 p.m., June,
July, and August, and Saturday and Sunday, 1:00 to 4:00 p.m.,
May, September, and October.

continues

Osceola and St. Croix Valley Railway
114 Depot Road
PO Box 176 (mailing address)
Osceola, WI 54020
715-755-3570
contact@mtmuseum.org
www.trainride.org/oscv.shtml

🛏 LODGING OPTIONS

Asa Parker House Bed and Breakfast
17500 St. Croix Trail North
Marine on St. Croix, MN 55047
651-433-5248 or 877-433-5248
asaparkerhouse@aol.com
www.bbonline.com/mn/asa

St. Croix River Inn
305 River Street
PO Box 356 (mailing address)
Osceola, WI 54020
715-294-4248 or 800-645-8820
innkeeper@stcroixriverinn.com
www.bbonline.com/wi/stcroixriver

See also Stillwater and Hudson for lodging options.

GREATER MARINE ON ST. CROIX TOUR

See map on p. 113.

Like Stillwater, one could call the entire village of Marine on St. Croix a historic district. And actually . . . it is! The good news is that, unlike the great city down the river, Marine on St. Croix is tiny. You can easily walk the entire village, an excellent idea considering how very narrow many of the lanes are on both the east and west side.

Marine on St. Croix has changed a great deal even since its nomination as a National Register District in 1974. Of the original boundaries of the historic district—Spruce Street, Kennedy Street, the Soo Line tracks, and the St. Croix River—only the river remains as a marker. Perhaps as a reflection of this change, the National Register no longer lists individual structures with addresses under its district designation for the city.

Let it be sufficient, then, to know that what remains is very worth looking at.

"NR" indicates National Register properties.

1. MARINE ON ST. CROIX NATIONAL REGISTER DISTRICT

Leave Highway 95 coming from the south at Judd Street to enter the village. If coming from the north, turn left at your first opportunity, which is Pine Street.

1a. MARINE MILL SITE (1839, NR)
Judd Street south of Maple Street

1b. MARINE FERRY LANDING
Foot of Elm Street

1c. MARINE TOWNSHIP HALL/STONE HOUSE MUSEUM (1872, NR)
241 5th Street, between Pine and Oak streets

The township hall is built of sandstone quarried and cut by a local mason. It was chosen by the National Historic American Buildings Survey in 1934 as an outstanding example of Swedish stonework of early Minnesota settlement days.

1d. MILL PONDS
Broadway at Rose Street

1e. HISTORIC RED BRIDGE (1885, REBUILT 1813)
Between Broadway and Rosabell streets, over the mill run

Judd Street, Marine Mills, 1902

1f. SITE OF THE GASKILL FLOURING MILL
Just east of the Red Bridge where Broadway and Maple meet 5th Street

1g. ASA PARKER HOUSE (1856, NR)
17500 St. Croix Trail North (Highway 95)

1h. OAKLAND CEMETERY (1872)
Broadway Street at Ostrum Trail

2. PACKER-HADRATH ESTATE/DUNROVIN RETREAT CENTER
15525 St. Croix Trail North (Highway 95), just north of 154th Street North

Built in the 1920s by Arthur and Clara Packer as the Morning Glory Trout and Game Preserve. Purchased by the Christian Brothers for a retreat site, today Dunrovin Retreat Center serves as a facility for adults and youth of many religious denominations, offering conference and retreat facilities, summer camps for inner-city children, and private cabins.

3. ST. CROIX WATERSHED RESEARCH STATION
16910 152nd Street North

Established in 1989, the SCWRS is the field research station of the Science Museum of Minnesota. The campus

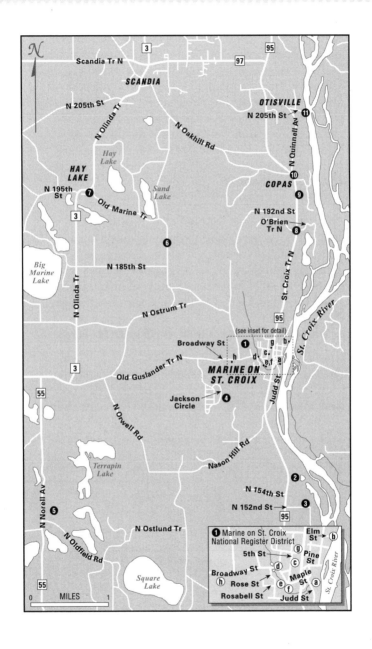

provides housing and laboratory facilities for researchers and a conference site for groups and organizations. The John Warner Grigg Dunn library holds most of the Minnesota historian James Taylor Dunn's collection of notes, photographs, and publications. The SCWRS sponsors the Artist at Pine Needles Residency Program for natural history artists and writers at the historic Pine Needles cabin once owned by James Taylor Dunn.

4. JACKSON MEADOW
2161 Jackson Circle

Take Broadway Street west out of Marine on St. Croix, and follow its curve south to the hilltop development site. A historically sensitive housing development designed by world-famous architect David Salmela, who received the 2005 American Institute of Architecture award for Urban Design and Planning for this project.

5. THE LEE AND ROSE WARNER NATURE CENTER (1965)
15375 Norell Avenue North

The oldest private nature center in Minnesota, Warner features over six hundred acres of undeveloped woodland, marsh, lake, bog, and grasslands. The center joined

Pine Needles, Dunn family cabin at Marine Mills, now owned by St. Croix Watershed Research Station

with other community partners in 2000 to create a greenway corridor over 2,400 acres (about four square miles) of protected land in the St. Croix River Valley.

6. THE OLD MARINE TRAIL (ESTABLISHED C. 1850)

Take Broadway Street west out of Marine on St. Croix, and turn north onto Ostrum Trail (County Road 4) and onto Old Marine Trail. The road ends at the historic Hay Lake Museum above the east bay of Marine Lake in New Scandia Township.

7. HAY LAKE SCHOOL (1896, NR) AND ERICKSON LOG HOUSE (1868, NR) MUSEUM
HAY LAKE MONUMENT TO THE FIRST SWEDISH IMMIGRANTS (1900)
14020 195th Street North

The log house was constructed by Swedish immigrant Johnannes Erickson and purchased by the Washington County Historical Society in 1974. Hay Lake School was used until 1963 and purchased by the Washington County Historical Society in 1978. Both historic structures were grouped around the 1900 Hay Lake Monument to form a museum complex.

8. WILLIAM O'BRIEN STATE PARK
16821 O'Brien Trail North

9. JOHN COPAS FARMHOUSE
19489 St. Croix Trail North (Highway 95), Copas

10. COPAS SCHOOLHOUSE (1875)
St. Croix Trail North (Highway 95) at 197th Street

11. LOG HOUSE LANDING
205th Street North east of Quinnell Avenue, Otisville

SCANDIA AND CHISAGO LAKES AREA

The Swedish emigration to North America in the nineteenth century, and particularly to Minnesota, is best depicted in the suite of novels by Swedish author Vilhelm Moberg. A great many of the Swedes who settled northern Washington County and Chisago County (later known to Swedes as "New Småland") and farmed and labored in the lumber mills or logged up north in the winter camps of the pineries came from the province of Småland, as well as Skåne and Varmland. The quality of life of these pioneers, with intense heat in summer and bitter cold in winter, was not unlike that in their homeland, and the landscape, with its rolling hills and rocky fields, also offered a sense of familiarity.

Their first years in Minnesota were stripped down to the most basic survival, but they stayed together in groups and established churches very quickly as a means of creating community. The Swedes were the most challenged by the English language, emigrating some twenty-five years after many settlers had arrived from New England, Ireland, and the United Kingdom. It took a full generation to move the Småland Swedes to English fluency, but in a relatively short period the men in particular were quick to learn the American way of life and politics and became leaders in their villages and townships.

Scandia, northwest of Marine Mills, had strong ties with the riverside town, as a great percentage of the steamboats coming upriver docked at the Marine Mills levee to permit hundreds of new immigrants to disembark. Log House Landing was also in steady use farther up the Minnesota shore. In the 1850s through the 1870s, a substantial percentage of the arrivals were Swedish, with Norwegians and Danes coming in much smaller numbers.

Scandia was the home of the first Swedish immigrants to settle in Minnesota. A second village grew up on the west side of Big Marine Lake, and by 1854 there were some forty Swedish families on the east side. These settlers, mostly immigrants from Småland, were able to move east to Scandia and north to the Swedish settlements by hacking oxcart paths through the heavy woods.

Olinda Trail (County Road 3) was the longest of these cart roads, taking those living in the south districts at Marine Lake and Hay Lake north to the three Swedish towns built on *Ki-chi-saga Sagi-a-gan* ("The Lovely Waters"): Lindström, Chisago City, and Center City.

The lovely waters proved to be a huge draw for tourism once automobiles and improved roads came to these lake cities. The resort era for the Chisago Lakes began in the 1880s with the building of grand hotels reached by train and halted with the Depression in the early 1930s. Visitors began flocking once again to the Chisago Lakes in the 1950s, but this time they came looking for summer homes and for year-round residences. Today, most of the summer cabins have been modernized into permanent homes, and the area's citizens commute into the Twin Cities for work on a daily basis.

Town Tennis Club outing at Hazelden Farms Lodge, 1936. The lodge was purchased by the Hazelden Foundation as a retreat and care center in 1949.

Vivid reminders of the immigrant past are everywhere: Swedish is used as often as English on exterior main street signage, and the many brightly painted Dalahäst horses point to where the old family names once came from.

Today, all twenty-two miles of Highway 8 are designated the Moberg Immigrant Trail.

ℹ️ LOCAL RESOURCES

Chisago County Historical Society
13100 3rd Avenue North
Lindström, MN 55045-9339
(651) 213-8550

City of Scandia
Scandia Community and Senior Center
14727 209th Street North
Scandia, MN 55047
651-433-2274
www.ci.scandia.mn.us/

Scandia Community Information
www.scandiamn.com

Gammelgården Museum
20880 Olinda Trail (County Road 3)
Scandia, MN 55047
651-433-5053
museum@gammelgardenmuseum.org
www.gammelgardenmuseum.org

Chisago Lakes Area Chamber of Commerce
30525 Linden Street
PO Box 283 (mailing address)
Lindström, MN 55045
651-257-1177
clacc@frontiernet.net
www.chisagolakeschamber.com

Center City Historical Society
313 Main Street North
PO Box 366 (mailing address)
Center City, MN 55012
651-257-6691

continues

Lindström Historical Society
PO Box 12
Lindström, MN 55045

Ki-Chi-Saga Park
29061 Glader Boulevard
Lindström, MN 55045
651-257-2519 or 651-464-3594

Swedish Circle Tours: Kichi-Saga
651-257-4773
www.swedishcircletours.com
Guided tours of eight area villages by prior arrangement.

LODGING OPTIONS

Country Bed and Breakfast
17038 320th Street
Shafer, MN 55074
651-257-4773
www.countrybedandbreakfast.us

Summit Inn Bed and Breakfast
208 Summit Avenue
PO Box 264 (mailing address)
Center City, MN 55012
651-257-4987
www.summitinnbb.com

Rose Hill Cabin Resort
30455 Lehigh Avenue
Lindström, MN 55045
651-257-4040
info@rosehillresort.com
www.rosehillresort.com

See also Taylors Falls, Osceola, and St. Croix Falls for lodging options.

SCANDIA AND CHISAGO LAKES AREA TOUR

See map on p. 121.

Minnesota's New Scandia Township and Greater Chisago Lakes Area, the Ki-chi-saga Sagi-a-gan historical lands, are considered the Swedish Circle. Comprised of eight communities—Scandia, Shafer, Lindström, Center City, Chisago City, Taylors Falls, Almelünd, and North Branch—all share the same Swedish immigrant roots.

"NR" indicates National Register properties.

1. HISTORIC SCANDIA
Olinda Trail at Oakhill Road

Take Scandia Trail (County Road 97) west from St. Croix Trail North (Highway 95) to Olinda Trail, and turn south into town. An entirely Swedish village with gaily painted traditional Dalahäst wooden horses hanging from every porch.

2. GAMMELGÅRDEN MUSEUM
20880 Olinda Trail, south of Oakhill Road

Gammelgården ("old small farm") Swedish Immigrant Museum is an eleven-acre site owned by Elim Lutheran Church, which since 1972 has preserved, presented, and promoted Swedish immigrant heritage and history.

3. SCANDIA ELIM CHURCH (1854)
Olinda Trail North at 205th Street North

4. ELIM CEMETERY (1860s)
Olinda Trail North at 205th Street North

The Swedish Sisters

Five Swedish settlements in New Scandia Township and on the chain of lakes just north in Chisago County have

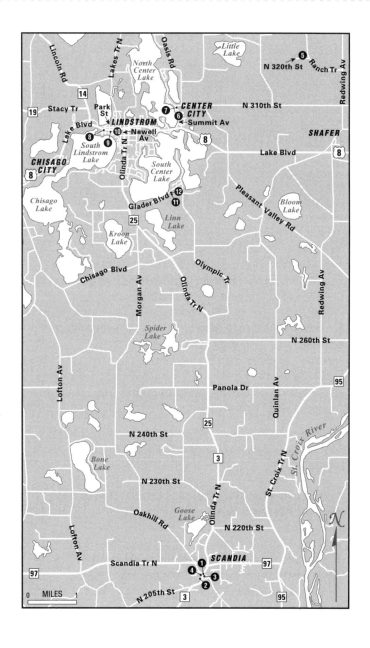

Scandia creamery, 1894

roots back to the 1850s. Each of the cities has a sister city in Sweden: Center City and Hassela, Chisago City and Algutsboda, Lindström and Tingsryd, Scandia and Lessebo Kommun, and Shafer and Nöbbele.

5. LARS THORSANDER HOUSE (TORSÅS BONDEGÅRD)/ COUNTRY BED AND BREAKFAST
17038 320th Street, Shafer

6. CENTER CITY HISTORIC DISTRICT (1800s, NR)
Summit Avenue, Center City

Center City is the Chisago County seat and the oldest continuously inhabited Swedish settlement in Minnesota.

7. CHISAGO LAKE EVANGELICAL CHURCH, CENTER CITY HISTORIC DISTRICT (1888, NR)
Summit Avenue, Center City

8. STATUES OF VILHELM MOBERG'S FICTIONAL IMMIGRANTS, KARL OSKAR AND KRISTINA NILSSON
Highway 8, Lindström

9. CHARLES VICTOR HOUSE (1905, NR)
30495 Park Street, Lindström

10. FRANK LARSON HOUSE, FRIDHEM ("HOME OF PEACE") (1898, NR)

Newell Avenue, Lindström

11. KARL OSKAR HOUSE, NYA DUVEMÅLA ("NEW DOVE'S HOME")

29061 Glader Boulevard, Lindström

From Lindström, go two miles south on Olinda Boulevard, take a left on Glader Boulevard, and go one mile to Kichi-Saga Park. Open Sunday afternoons, May thru September.

12. GLADER PIONEER CEMETERY (1850)

Glader Boulevard just east of Kichi-Saga Park, Lindström

Oldest Lutheran Cemetery in Chisago County and the oldest Swedish cemetery in Minnesota. Chosen by Wilhelm Moberg as the fictional burial site for Karl Oskar and Kristina in the film of his novel *The Emigrants.*

Swedish Evangelical Lutheran Church, Center City, 1894

FRANCONIA

Travelers may wish to take advantage of the Osceola Bridge to cross the St. Croix to Osceola, Wisconsin. From St. Croix Trail North (Highway 95) take the exit east onto State Highway 243 (the shortest state highway in Minnesota) over the river into downtown Osceola. You may travel north to St. Croix Falls/Interstate State Park and cross back into Taylors Falls, Minnesota, via the Highway 8 bridge and then come down to Franconia from the north. From the south, turn down Franconia Trail just before reaching Highway 8.

Located some three miles downriver from Taylors Falls, below the Dalles and around Lawrence Creek, Franconia was first settled by Ansel Smith, a teacher from St. Croix Falls who, in 1852, began clearing the forested land near the river to make space for a 16-by-26-foot shanty and a large garden. Smith had named the little community for his home near Franconia Notch in the White Mountains of New Hampshire. He put in a stock of goods for possible river trade but realized very little from his investment. Franconia was platted on the rise above the river by Smith in 1858, and the tiny community began developing, with houses being built along Lawrence Creek and up the hillside; businesses—two hotels, two stores, three saloons, and a blacksmith shop—opened down toward the mill on the river flats.

The Civil War came to Franconia as elsewhere in the St. Croix Valley. Henry Day enlisted in the Seventh Minnesota Regiment, Company C, until his honorable discharge at Memphis, Tennessee, in 1865. On his return home to Franconia, he married local schoolteacher Margaret Smith and built a house near his brother's. Paul Munch, an immigrant from Luxembourg and at that time a carpenter in Taylors Falls, enlisted in the First Minnesota Light Artillery Battery and, upon his return to Minnesota in 1865, relocated to Franconia. Eric Ostrōm, a Swedish immigrant in 1861, almost immediately upon his arrival at Franconia enlisted to serve. Jonas Lindall (Johannes Lindahl), who had arrived in Franconia the year before, became an officer in Company D of the Third Minnesota Regiment.

From 1861 to 1865, the partnership of White, Thornton, and Irish built steamboats and barges at Franconia, including the *Jenny Thornton,* the *Ben Campbell,* the *Jenny Hayes,* the *Gracie Kent,* and the sidewheeler the *Viola.*

Paul Munch established the Franconia Flour Mill, a three-story structure built of stone on Lawrence Creek, upon his return from the war in 1865. He constructed a two-story warehouse the following year. Henry Vitalis, a Swedish immigrant, came to clerk for Munch in 1868. And Ansel Smith, after fifteen years in Franconia, was appointed receiver of the U.S. Land Office at Duluth and departed to take up his new duties.

Perhaps it was the great disappointment that the railroad being put in from St. Paul to Duluth had bypassed Franconia in 1878 and the news the same year that pioneer founder Ansel Smith had died in Duluth. It could have been the floods of 1879 that washed away the flour mill dams and undermined the buildings' foundations. Maybe it was the creamery burning down. But most likely it was the St. Croix Boom Company's total domination and its lack of effort to keep the steamboat channel open that spelled the end of business for the timber and flouring mills above Stillwater and, therefore, Franconia.

The village tried to hang on, and a new hotel, the Franconia, was built in 1882. But more and more of the village's population was departing, lock, stock, and house. Residential structures were moved by horse teams west to Shafer, Lindström, and Center City. One house was placed on skids and hauled across the ice to Osceola. The Franconia Hotel itself was carried up to the top of the bluff in 1892, where it continued operations as a guesthouse. The last general store closed in 1898, and the village became a district of empty lots and silent streets, with just a few families staying on in this once idyllic spot on the St. Croix. Franconia became a ghost town.

Hotel and saloon, Franconia, c1900

ⓘ LOCAL RESOURCES

Chisago County Historical Society
13100 3rd Avenue North
Lindström, MN 55045-9339
(651) 213-8550

Falls Chamber of Commerce
715-483-3580
director@fallschamber.org
www.fallschamber.org

Franconia Sculpture Park
29836 St. Croix Trail North (Highway 95)
Franconia, MN 55074
651-257-6668
info@franconia.org
tours@franconia.org
www.franconia.org
Free and open daily dawn to dusk.

See Marine on St. Croix, Osceola, Taylors Falls, and St. Croix Falls for lodging options.

FRANCONIA TOUR

See map on p. 129.

Travelers may see many beautiful sites and cities along the St. Croix but few like Franconia winding down the narrow lane off of Highway 95. We are greatly fortunate to have an excellent series of photographs at the Minnesota Historical Society taken in the village's heyday, and many in the years after its end, when the Vitalis family seemed to be the only remaining residents and the Vitalis children played along abandoned wooden walkways and empty lots.

Franconia became a National Historic District, and its preservation in its current form is assured. Half of its riverfront acreage is now gone: only Summer Street extends beyond the last north-south passage of Henry Street. Also gone is Mill Street, which ran for two blocks to the north of Summer Street and was the site of a store, a stable, and a hotel, and Main Street, which was once the extension of the Franconia Trail where the Clarke house and a creamery stood. The town hall survived because it was moved from its site on Cornelian Street up to the top of the bluff.

1. STEAMBOAT LANDING SITE
Bottom of Summer Street at the St. Croix River

2. FRANCONIA FLOUR MILL AND MILLRACE SITE
Summer Street at Franconia Trail (Lawrence Creek)

3. PAUL MUNCH HOUSE
Summer Street

4. CHARLES VITALIS HOUSE
Cornelian Boulevard

5. JOHNSON HOUSE
Edward Boulevard

6. FRANCONIA HISTORIC MARKER
Summer Street

7. SWANLUND HOUSE
Wolf Road at Edward Boulevard

8. HANSON HOUSE
Henry Boulevard at Wolf Road

9. FRANCONIA CEMETERY
297th Street North

Take Lawrence Creek Road off Highway 95 near its intersection at Highway 8. Road closed to automobile traffic. Cemetery records at Chisago County Historical Society.

10. FRANCONIA TOWN HALL (C. 1880)
25156 St. Croix Trail North (Highway 95) at Redwing Avenue North (County Road 86)

11. FRANCONIA SCULPTURE PARK
29836 St. Croix Trail North (Highway 95) at Highway 8

Artists are invited every year to create and display their work during a residency supported by Minnesota's Jerome Foundation Fellowship Program. The park hosts twenty-five artists and ten artist interns yearly. Free and open to the public daily from dawn to dusk.

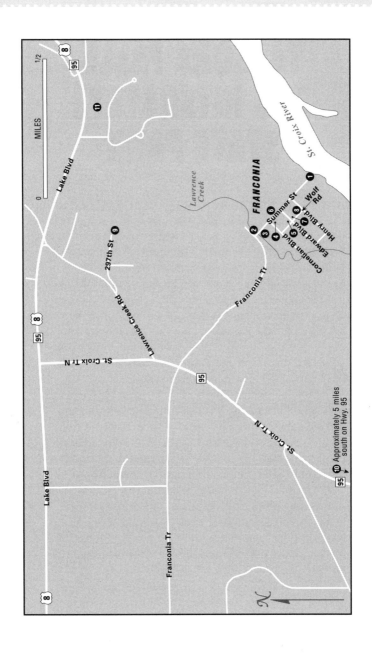

TAYLORS FALLS AND INTERSTATE STATE PARK

Jesse Taylor, a stonemason, came here in 1838 to establish timber claims. The site where he built a shanty was first called Taylor's Place. Taylor was working at the most southerly edge of the great white pine district, an area with extraordinary waterpower potential (*Menominikeshi Kakabikang,* or The Falls of the Ricebird River) that had not been given much attention. His claim wasn't the easiest to defend: he was under instruction from Fort Snelling to make the claim and found a French Canadian in possession of the desirable tract of land. How he dispossessed the unfortunate prior claimant is unknown, but he was able to secure the woodland.

Jesse Taylor and a partner, B. F. Baker, proceeded to build a mill, the Baker's Falls Company, and milldam in 1839, along with a blacksmith shop. Baker's Falls became the new name for the site. Baker died unexpectedly in St. Louis the following year, and without the substantial capital he had brought to the partnership, Taylor had no choice but to abandon the mill site and transfer the property to Joshua L. Taylor (no relation). It was then preempted in 1849 by Joshua Taylor and Nathan C. D. Taylor (still no relation)—which fixed for the future the name of the site as Taylor's Falls (apostrophe included).

Jesse Taylor stayed on at the old log shanty, selling off machinery and tools from the millworks. The mill building itself was sold and moved across the river to Osceola. The shop buildings were burned and the land cleared. The log shanty (supposedly haunted by ghosts) stayed on, serving in turn as a storehouse, mercantile, saloon, post office, carpenter's shop, and church, eventually becoming the town's first schoolhouse until a proper structure could be built in 1853.

Benjamin Otis and his Ojibwe wife, Mary, settled here in 1846 and built a house. W. H. C. Folsom arrived at Taylor's Falls in 1850 to build the first frame building for a store and residence. This store was a success.

Ansel Smith and Samuel Thomson came in 1851 to build the Chisago House (later the Dalles House) for lumbermen and river travelers. The large structure offered twenty rooms, a sample room for traveling salesmen and traders, an office, a parlor, a dining room, a kitchen, and storerooms. This hotel would change hands almost continuously over the next twenty-five years.

The first plat surveys for the development of town lots were undertaken in 1851 by Theodore S. Parker. Ansel Smith built a house for himself that same year but, in 1852, following the death of his young daughter, moved downriver with the Otis family to lay out a new town to be called Otisville.

After Chisago County was organized in January 1852, Taylor's Falls successfully lobbied to be designated the county seat. With the promotion of community status in mind, W. H. C. Folsom built a new hotel, the Union House, in 1852. It too would pass through many hands over the next twenty-three years. A smaller hostel, the Union House offered twelve rooms, a parlor, an office, a dining room, and a kitchen.

More arrivals came to settle at Taylor's Falls, including George Folsom and also Richard Arnold, who built the Cascade House in 1853. The private, nondenominational Kahbakong Cemetery Association was organized in 1853 a mile and a half north of the town: W. H. C. Folsom, seemingly everywhere, was its first president. The St. Croix Bridge Company received a charter to build in the spring of 1854, and a graceful wooden arched bridge went up in 1856, connecting Taylor's Falls to its neighbor across the river, St. Croix Falls. Levi Folsom, an attorney, and his wife, Abby, came to settle in the new town.

Taylor's Falls was incorporated in 1859, and among its first officers were W. H. C. and Levi Folsom. A charter was granted by the state legislature in 1857 to build a school for higher education to be based in Taylor's Falls. Named the Chisago Seminary, it was constructed by the peripatetic W. H. C. Folsom, who secured permission for the new academy to be operated as a public institution rather than as a private school. It was built that same year and opened with its first class of sixty students, teaching the classics and modern languages.

With the firing on Fort Sumter in April 1861 and President Lincoln's call for volunteer regiments to put down the southern rebellion, many of the men of the Taylor's Falls community went to war. This turn of events was the undoing of the Chisago Seminary, only four years in existence. At the outbreak of the war, most of the young men, together with the principal, Professor A. A. York, enlisted in 1861. The seminary did not

Taylor's Falls, 1869. The apostrophe was officially dropped after World War II.

survive the war years and closed in 1864, just months before Lee's surrender at Appomattox.

The years following the end of the war brought mixed blessings for Taylor's Falls. The Chisago Mill built by L. Kingman and Company in 1856 and purchased and improved by W. H. C. Folsom in 1858, was by 1875 in the ownership of Andrew Holtman, who ran the mill for several years and then, after failing to pay his taxes, hired a gang of men to come in during the middle of a moonless night and remove all the machinery except the boilers. What remained of the mill fell into decay.

The Nimokogan (Namekagon) and Totogatic Dam Company was organized in 1869; in 1870, its name was changed to the St. Croix Dam Company, and a new charter was granted, permitting the number of dams to be enlarged from two to nine and then again to twelve. The dam was designed to greatly facilitate log driving at forty cents per thousand feet of timber. The company was soon passing from forty to sixty million feet annually.

The late 1870s found Taylor's Falls as a full-service community with every possible amenity required for civilized town life. The railroad had come through, and a handsome depot was built. The Union House had doubled in size, and the new Falls Hotel opened in 1880. The school district had taken over the old Chisago Seminary building for a new city school and built a second educational institution on the north end of the growing town in 1870. And the wealthy had continued to construct great and handsome houses in the city, many now clustered along the old military road atop Angel Hill above the depot.

Suddenly, lumbering—as with the fate of Marine Mills—moved into uncertain times. Several seasons of very low water on both the St. Croix River and its tributaries made it impossible to raft logs down to sawmills. In just a few years, Taylor's Falls mills were in bankruptcy, the buildings abandoned and the millhands and lumbermen left without work on both sides of the river, from north to south. The sawmills were torn down in the 1890s, and Taylor's Falls was no longer a lumber town. Life went on, but by the time the new century had come, the population had dropped dramatically, with many houses and not a few of the commercial buildings and hotels abandoned.

Tourism started rising as an important source of income. The automobile and greatly improved roads began the steady stream of summer visitors from St. Paul and Minneapolis. Taylor's Falls' siting on the dramatic geological formations called the Dalles (Ojibwe, *Wibudjiwanong,* or the Rapids at the Contraction of the River) began to attract increasing numbers of sightseers every year. Small cabin resorts were built for summer visitors, and some of the old hotels were refurbished and reopened. Taylor's Falls was greatly aided by the improvement of Highway 8 stretching from old Highway 61 (now Interstate 35) through the Chisago Lakes to the St. Croix River. When the Depression came, the Civilian Conservation Corps was active in the area, particularly in the development of a new state park, called Interstate, to be jointly owned by the natural resources divisions of Minnesota and Wisconsin.

Dalles House, Taylor's Falls, 1895

Following World War II, town residents petitioned the legislature to permit the apostrophe in the town's name to be dropped. Taylor's Falls became Taylors Falls ever after.

After many historic buildings downriver at Marine on St. Croix were bulldozed, the Taylors Falls community organized to protect their heritage sites. Though rail service ended in 1960, Taylors Falls was now very much on the radar for summer vacationers, and an increasing number of year-round residents were buying and restoring many of the town's old and lovely houses. Others were building cabins on the shore outside of town for summer homes.

Chimney Rock, St. Croix Dalles at Taylor's Falls, c1870

In the late 1960s, the Minnesota Historical Society commissioned a complete historic sites survey of Taylors Falls. By 1970, the society had placed Taylors Falls' Angel Hill on the National Register as a historic district—a total of thirty-four properties—and also had several individual structures placed on the National Register as historic places in 1970 and 1980. Research into many other Taylors Falls buildings continues.

Natural wells, St. Croix Dalles at Taylor's Falls, c1890

Today visitors arrive by car and tour bus, bicycle and motorcycle. They walk the streets of the business district, drive up past the old depot to see the great beauty of the white houses on Angel Hill, and picnic in Interstate State Park and go exploring among the fascinating geological formations that make up the Dalles. The paddlewheelers *Taylors Falls Queen* and *Taylors Falls*

Princess may take them down through the magnificent Dalles with knowledgeable guides, or they may sign on for guided canoe trips down to Osceola or up the Wild River.

 LOCAL RESOURCES

Falls Chamber of Commerce
715-483-3580
director@fallschamber.org
www.fallschamber.org

St. Croix Valley Group Tours
106 Washington Street
St. Croix Falls, WI 54024
651-451-6315 or 800-447-4958
tour@scfwi.com
www.fallschamber.org

City of Taylors Falls
637 1st Street
Taylors Falls, MN 55084
651-465-5133
tfclerk@frontiernet.net
www.taylorsfalls.govoffice.com

Taylors Falls Historical Society
Folsom House
272 West Government Street
Taylors Falls, MN 55084
651-465-3125
folsomhouse@mnhs.org
www.mnhs.org/places/sites/fh
Open daily, 1:00 to 4:30 p.m., except Tuesdays.
Small admission fee; group reservations welcome.

Interstate State Park/Minnesota
307 Milltown Road
Taylors Falls, MN 55084
651-465-5711
www.dnr.state.mn.us/state_parks/interstate

continues

Interstate State Park/Wisconsin
State Highway 35
PO Box 703
St. Croix Falls, WI 54024
715-483-3747
www.dnr.state.wi.us/org/LAND/parks/specific/interstate

**St. Croix National Scenic Riverway Visitor Center,
National Park Service**
401 North Hamilton Street
St. Croix Falls, WI 54024
715-483-2274
www.nps.gov/sacn

Taylors Falls Scenic Boat Tours
Box 235
Taylors Falls, MN 55084
651-465-6315 or 800-447-4958
boats@wildmountain.com
www.taylorsfallsboat.com
Daily 1½-hour scenic cruises May thru October. Private
charters available. Many specialty cruises scheduled.

Wild River Canoe Rental
Highway 8 at Highway 35 (across from Polk County Visitor Center)
St. Croix Falls, WI 54024
651-270-1561
www.ericscanoerental.com
Guided canoe trips south through the Dalles to Osceola,
or north to the Wild River. Shuttle service.

LODGING OPTIONS

Cottage Bed and Breakfast
950 Fox Glen Drive
Taylors Falls, MN 55084
651-465-3595
cottage12@frontiernet.net
www.the-cottage.com

*See also Marine on St. Croix, Osceola, St. Croix Falls,
and Dresser for lodging options.*

TAYLORS FALLS AND INTERSTATE STATE PARK TOUR

See map on p. 139.

"NR" indicates National Register properties.

1. MILLTOWN SITE
Milltown Road off highways 95 and 8

The ruins of an early settlement found at the time of the first survey of the Taylors Falls site in 1851, located at a hamlet called Milltown down the shore from the falls. The ruins of an old chimney and other traces of occupation point to a trading post connected with the St. Croix Trail up to La Pointe, Wisconsin.

2. INTERSTATE PARK STATE / MINNESOTA (1938, NR) AND WISCONSIN
Off Highway 8, west side of bridge

Interstate State Park, which lies on both sides of the St. Croix River, has its greatest number of National Register structures on the Minnesota side, built by the Civilian Conservation Corps of the 1930s, now under National Register protection. In Minnesota, Interstate is the second-oldest state park. The Wisconsin side is that state's oldest state park and has the greatest percentage of parklands and river views of the spectacular Wisconsin Dalles.

3. INTERSTATE STATE PARK / WISCONSIN
Off Highway 8 after crossing bridge to St. Croix Falls

4. MUNCH-ROOS HOUSE (1853, NR)
360 Bench Street

Greek Revival frame dwelling built by the Luxembourger immigrant Munch brothers as a residence and carpenter shop. (See also Munch House, p. 127.)

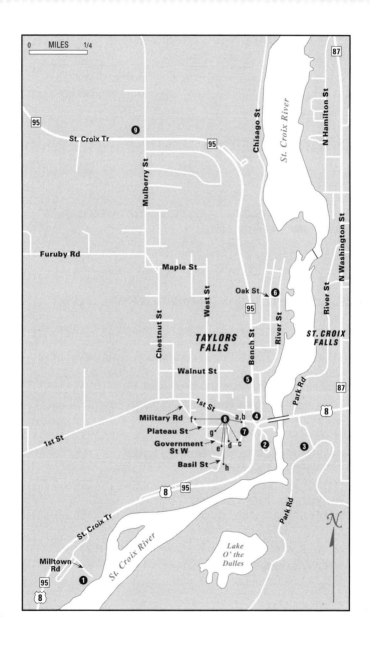

5. TAYLORS FALLS PUBLIC LIBRARY (1854, NR)
473 Bench Street

Eastlake-style frame residence and tailor shop designed by John Jacob Spengler, later acquired by city for use as a public library.

6. JOHN DAUBNEY HOUSE (1870, NR)
Oak and River streets

An Italianate frame house.

7. NORTHERN PACIFIC RAILROAD DEPOT/TAYLORS FALLS COMMUNITY CENTER (1902)
312 Government Street

Managed by the City of Taylors Falls. Call 651-465-5133.

8. ANGEL HILL NATIONAL REGISTER HISTORIC DISTRICT

A hilltop community of distinctive white nineteenth-century frame residences, public buildings, and churches reminiscent of New England villages. The name *Angel Hill* refers to the church steeple atop the hill. Most houses are of white pine in the Greek Revival style. Government Street and Military Road are the northern extension of the Point Douglas–Superior government road.

8a. SCHOTTMULLER BREWERY (1851, NR)
100 West Government Street

8b. VILLAGE JAIL (N. D. , NR)
102 West Government Street

8c. W. H. C. FOLSOM HOUSE / TAYLORS FALLS HISTORICAL SOCIETY (1854, NR)
272 West Government Street

8d. FIRST METHODIST CHURCH (1861, NR)
290 West Government Street

Open 10:00 a.m. Sundays for worship services

8e. FIRST SCHOOLHOUSE AND COMMUNITY CENTER (1852, NR)
331 West Government Street

8f. METHODIST PARSONAGE (1865, NR)
366 Military Road

8g. NEVERS HOUSE (1869, NR)
361 Plateau Street

8h. LEVI FOLSOM HOUSE (1856, NR)
212 Basil Street

9. KAHBAKONG CEMETERY (1855)
Highway 95 and County Road 71

One of the largest and oldest cemeteries in Chisago County. W. H. C. Folsom founded and named this cemetery and is buried here. The cemetery holds burials of sixty-seven Civil War veterans. Its name is from the Ojibwe *Menominikeshi Kakabikang* ("The Falls of the Ricebird River").

W. H. C. Folsom's house, Taylor's Falls, c1860

Wisconsin Central Railroad bridge over St. Croix River, 1909

WISCONSIN

PRESCOTT

This point of land at the bottom of Lake St. Croix—at its confluence with the Mississippi (in Dakota, *O-Ki-Źu Wa-Kpá,* or Where River Water Gathers into a Lake)— was a campsite for Zebulon Pike in 1805 when he was sent up the Mississippi to drive out British traders. A dozen years afterward, the site was reviewed by Stephen Long as a possible location for a military post, but the higher bluffs upstream seemed a better location for what became Fort Snelling.

Philander Prescott, a St. Paul merchant and a Dakota interpreter for the U.S. government, was offered the site in 1838 by the fort's officers as an ideal place for a trading post. Prescott and his Dakota wife, Mary (originally Nag-He-No-Wenah, or Spirit in the Moon), kept his trading post through a decade of hard times, eventually hiring the French Canadian trader Joseph Monjeau (Mozhoe) of Point Douglas to live in the cabin and run the post. Prescott's namesake town would rarely see him again.

Steamboats brought new settlers and their families, along with supplies and machinery, several hotels, a boat levee, warehouses, and many new businesses and houses up the hill from the landing, just across the river from its sister city, Hastings, Minnesota.

Prescott was organized in 1851 and its city charter granted in 1857. By the late 1850s, millers were shipping 3,000 bushels of wheat out of the town, and the city levee was one long line of storage and mercantile structures built to serve steamboat arrival, construct more boats, and provide for the needs of the growing population. It was remarkable that Prescott, a quarter the size of Stillwater, could boast double the number of lumber and flour mills.

The levee was constantly being expanded and upgraded with fill from the Kinnickinnic riverbanks to permit many steamboats to land and unload daily. A ferry had been established between Prescott and Point Douglas as early as 1840. A scheduled steam ferry began business in the mid-1850s for passengers, carts, and the shipping of goods and supplies between Prescott and both Hastings and Point Douglas.

The Civil War muster rolls for the first, sixth, twelfth, twentieth, thirtieth, and thirty-seventh regiments of the Wisconsin volunteer infantry show the enlistment of over 130 men from Prescott. The Prescott Guards, who had been organized in late 1860, were ready for service immediately in 1861 and made up of lumbermen, millhands, store clerks, craftsmen, and workers of many other trades.

On their departure from their home town to the fort, the Guards were easily seen for the bright red shirts they wore. Companies continued to form through war years, and new militia units began training maneuvers, including the Banner Badgers, the Prescott artillery unit. Company A of the Twelfth Wisconsin Regiment had the largest number of Prescott men. And owing to a large population of African Americans in the surrounding townships, many Prescott-area men enlisted in the U.S. Colored Troops regiments and received veteran commendations and burials upon returning home.

In 1862, news came to Prescott that the city's namesake, Philander Prescott, had died at Fort Ridgely during the U.S.–Dakota War, a short but bloody clash between Minnesota river settlements and Dakota people brought to starvation when government annuity payments were greatly delayed.

The city hummed along in the years after the war. The railroad came through in the 1880s at the height of the lumber milling era, offering a new year-round land-shipping alternative to steamboats. But by the turn of the century, the railroad dominated Prescott's economic life, as it did in Hastings, and the lumber industry had declined.

In 1889, a massive logjam upriver sparked an idea that gave some hope. A new log boom was built on the bay across from Prescott. Funded by the St. Paul Boom Company, based in Prescott, it received log rafts and also the many stray logs that continued to float downriver, each branded with a company symbol and returned to its owner for a bounty. But finally, the logging industry died away. As the cleanup of drift logs continued, they were gathered at the Prescott boom. A few stray logs remained in the boom for two years before they were finally sent down the Mississippi; it was believed to be the last raft of logs to pass through the Point Douglas bay.

Road improvements and automobiles—the first autos seen in Prescott arrived in 1903—caused the Prescott City Council to take notice of new possibilities for the small town, which was looking for additional commercial support. The Prescott Bridge Company was formed in 1920 to organize a span over the St. Croix that would connect with Point Douglas on the Minnesota side of the river. Work was begun on a steel truss span with a center sixty-foot vertical lift, and the bridge officially opened in 1923. Tolls were set for all conveyances—automobiles, wagons, bicycles, and motorcycles—at twenty-five cents per vehicle and five cents for each passenger, with a thirty-five-cent maximum toll.

Traffic was light in the first two decades but steadily increased after World War II, and the two states on either

Main Street, Prescott, c1910

Lift toll bridge at Prescott-Hastings, 1920

side of the lift bridge negotiated to purchase the privately financed span from the Prescott Bridge Company and to permit free passage. Eventually replaced with a new bridge in 1990, the old one was scrapped, but the restored gear house from the original, which had to be operated manually, now sits in Mercord Mill Park.

Today, like many of the other historic towns on the St. Croix River, Prescott has worked to promote its nineteenth-century commercial and residential buildings, the historic quality of its main street, and its ties to the rivers. Prescott is home to the Great River Road Visitor and Education Center, which overlooks the confluence of the St. Croix and Mississippi rivers from Freedom Park. The park offers programs and exhibits about the history of early peoples, historic settlements, and current ecology issues. Many visitors come to watch the eagles and falcons floating on the thermals above the rivers.

🛈 LOCAL RESOURCES

Prescott Heritage and Welcome Center
233 Broad Street
Prescott, WI 54021
715-262-3284
www.pressenter.com/~whctr

Prescott Area Chamber of Commerce
279 Broad Street North
Prescott, WI 54021
715-262-3284
info@prescottwi.com
www.prescottwi.com

City of Prescott
800 Borner Street
Prescott, WI 54021
715-262-5544
www.prescottwi.org

Great River Road Visitor and Learning Center
200 Monroe Street
Prescott, WI 54021
715-262-0104
www.freedomparkwi.org
Farmers' market open June thru October, Thursdays 3:00
to 7:00 p.m.

See also Hastings for local resources.

🛌 LODGING OPTIONS

The Arbor Bed and Breakfast Inn
434 North Court Street
Prescott, WI 54021
715-262-2222 or 888-262-1090
relax@thearborinn.com
www.thearborinn.com

See also Hastings, River Falls, and Afton for lodging options.

PRESCOTT TOUR

1. H. S. MILLER BANK BUILDING (1885, NR), PRESCOTT HERITAGE AND WELCOME CENTER
233 Broad Street

Travel information and maps are available at the center, along with displays depicting aspects of the fascinating history of Prescott.

2. PRESCOTT SPINNER FACTORY BUILDING (1928)
207 Broad Street

The Prescott Spinner Factory made fishing gear.

3. ST. JOSEPH'S CATHOLIC CHURCH (1912)
269 South Dakota Street

4. HARNESS SHOP (1883)
122 Orange Street

5. MERCORD MILL PARK

The site of the Mercord Sawmill (1852), later used as a flouring mill. The 1912 gear house from the historic lift bridge was moved here when the bridge was torn down for replacement.

RIVER FALLS AND THE KINNICKINNIC RIVER

Joel Foster, a Mexican-American War veteran, is credited as the first European settler at River Falls. In the winter of 1848 to 1849, he and his twenty-year-old African American indentured servant, Dick, built a log cabin along the banks of the Kinnickinnic River (in Dakota and Potawatomi, *Kinnikinnik Zibi,* the Tobacco or Toasted Red Willow Bark River), about a half mile south of the falls. They had come upriver from St. Louis looking for a more healthful climate, disembarked at Stillwater, crossed the lake to scout the falls up on the Willow River where Hudson would eventually develop, and walked a trail some twenty miles southeast to the town's namesake falls.

Foster's town developed with waterpower providing the drive behind both a sawmill and a flour mill, and the Kinnickinnic allowed passage upriver to the town from Lake St. Croix. The mill was prosperous, but what put the town on the map was the establishment of a state teacher's college, the River Falls Normal School, in 1874. The college made the town a locus of cultural and academic life, and as the campus expanded, so did the city. The Kinnickinnic River, which flows through River Falls, has become the heart of a lovely parkland that provides the community with considerable green space.

South Hall, State Normal School
(Teachers College), River Falls, 1915

🛈 LOCAL RESOURCES

City of River Falls
222 Lewis Street
River Falls, WI 54022
715-425-0900
kmckahan@rfcity.org
www.rfcity.org

**River Falls Area Chamber of Commerce
and Tourism Bureau**
214 North Main Street
River Falls, WI 54022
715-425-2533
www.rfchamber.com

Kinnickinnic State Park
W11983 820th Avenue
River Falls, WI 54022
715-425-1129
http://dnr.wi.gov/org/land/parks/specific/kinnickinnic

🛏 LODGING OPTIONS

The Servant Quarters Bed and Breakfast
N7249 910th Street
River Falls, WI 54022
715-425-8333
www.theservantquarters.com

Best Western River Falls Hotel and Suites
100 Spring Street
River Falls, WI 54022
715-425-1045
www.bestwesternwisconsin.com

See also Hudson, Prescott, and Hastings for lodging options.

RIVER FALLS TOUR

"NR" indicates National Register properties.

1. SOUTH HALL, RIVER FALLS STATE NORMAL SCHOOL (1900, NR)
NORTH HALL, RIVER FALLS STATE NORMAL SCHOOL (1914, NR)
East Cascade Street

The first building housing the River Falls Normal School was built in 1874 after the end of the Civil War, a seminary dedicated to preparing scholars for teaching careers. The original academy building burned and was rebuilt in 1900. The Normal School came to dominate River Falls in the years after World War I; it was renamed River Falls State Teachers School in 1927. From 1951 to 1964, the school was called Wisconsin State College–River Falls; in 1964, it became Wisconsin State University–River Falls. The school joined the University of Wisconsin system and was renamed University of Wisconsin–River Falls in 1971, when the former University of Wisconsin and the Wisconsin State Universities merged.

2. GLADSTONE HOTEL BUILDING (1886)
125 South Main Street

3. FALLS THEATER (1927)
105 South Main Street

4. GLEN PARK (1898)
West Park Street at Glen Park Road

A twenty-one-acre city park that once had a small zoo and still has a Civilian Conservation Corps swimming pool. A path leads from the upper park to the base of Junction Falls and the east bank of the Kinnickinnic River, known as the Glen.

5. JUNCTION MILL SITE
South Falls Road at Winter Street

Junction Mill, built by pioneer C. B. "Charley" Cox in 1867 at the top of the falls, was one of the city's first grist mills. It helped River Falls become a major producer of fine flour after the Civil War but burned down in 1897.

6. MUNICIPAL POWER PLANT AND DAM (1900)
West of Winter Street Bridge near Junction Falls

River Falls built a city power plant at this site in 1900 and added a diesel generator in 1923. The falls still generate 315 kilowatt-hours of hydropower.

7. RIVER FALLS METHODIST CHURCH (1897)
2nd Street and Walnut Street

8. KINNICKINNIC STATE PARK
County Road F, six miles west of town

The Kinnickinnic River begins with a beautiful sand delta on the St. Croix River. The valley of the Kinnickinnic, a cold-water trout stream, is a rare sanctuary with majestic white pines and sheer limestone cliffs and a haven for a great range of wildlife and more than 140 species of birds during the migrating season. The upland portions of the 1,242-acre park are being restored to prairie plants that flourished before European settlers arrived with their horses and plows.

9. ROSCIUS AND LYDIA FREEMAN HOUSE (1908, NR)
220 3rd Street

HUDSON AND THE WILLOW RIVER

The French Canadians arrived first in 1840, as they did on many sites along Lake St. Croix. Peter Bouchea, a French Ojibwe trader, and his brother-in-law Louis Massey paddled their canoes up the Willow River (a translation of the Dakota name *Ga-Ossissigobimijika Zibi),* settling in the vicinity of present-day 1st and St. Croix streets. Louis Massey married an Ojibwe woman from a nearby encampment up the river, and the families built rough dugouts for shelter. Fellow French Canadians William Steets and Joseph LeGrew soon joined them. The settlers lived chiefly by hunting and fishing and raising garden crops. Their compound was surrounded by a tall picket fence, which served as protection and an early warning system against unwanted visitors.

Within the next five years, more settlers arrived at this pleasant spot on the lake, including Rev. Lemuel Nobles's family and French Canadian Moses Perrin. William Nobles started a ferry service across the lake in 1848, and Moses Perrin, resettling from Lakeland, built a hotel and a boardinghouse adjacent to a livery stable.

Joel Foster, just returned from the battle of Buena Vista in 1848, suggested this as a new name for the town because of the fine view from the bluffs over the lake. Foster did not stay in the Buena Vista community but instead traveled south to the Kinnickinnic River falls and laid out a new town, Greenwood, in 1848. Greenwood would later become River Falls.

O. J. Henning petitioned the legislature in 1851 to change Buena Vista to a new name, Willow River, and platted the town. In 1852, Mayor Alfred Day petitioned to have the town's name changed one more time, to Hudson, as many steamboat travelers and lumbermen from New England saw a strong resemblance to the Hudson River in upstate New York. Hudson became the county seat of St. Croix County in 1853, built a schoolhouse in 1855, and was incorporated as a city in 1857.

Three banks were organized in the 1850s, and all closed within a year of their opening due to the panic of 1857. A fourth and fifth bank opened after the Civil War and endured and prospered. The following two decades saw considerable growth in Hudson, and lumbering was the center of its industry, as it was in every town up and down the St. Croix.

The railroad came through in 1871, providing direct overland transportation for passengers and shipping year-round. The largest of the sawmills, the Hudson, became the center of industrial operations in the town. A significant number of flouring mills were also built along the Willow River. Hudson continued to grow through the 1880s, the golden decade of the timber industry on the river, and with it so did the wealth of many of its citizens. This prosperity translated into some exceptionally beautiful residences and also investment in handsome commercial buildings in the business center of town. Lake Mallalieu, the vast millpond formed

View of Hudson, c1885

upstream within the city limits, became lined with ornamental boathouses and attractive landscaping.

Two fires, in 1866 and 1872, wiped out most of the business community and many of the town's residential structures. Large commercial blocks were rebuilt several times before the end of the century. A hotel, the Chapin Hall, burned in 1862, was rebuilt in 1868, and was lost to fire a second time in 1872. Undaunted, the owners rebuilt once more in 1879, and the leading citizens of Hudson supported the building of more fine commercial blocks and buildings. These two town fires prompted organization of the Hudson City Fire Company, with new fire engines and a centrally located engine house.

A private hospital was planned in 1886 by a specialist in nervous and mental diseases, Dr. Irving D. Wiltrout of Hudson. The sanatorium, built on Lake Mallalieu, was a large structure in the Queen Anne style by the well-known Minneapolis architect L. S. Buffington. Buffington ensured that the most up-to-date conveniences would be found in the hospital, including incandescent lighting and a modern heat and ventilation system. The new sanatorium was named the Oliver Wendell Holmes Hospital, and Holmes came in person to deliver

Oliver Wendell Holmes Hospital, Lake Mallalieu, Hudson, c1888

a dedication. Holmes, who had seen considerable action during the Civil War and was very familiar with the effects of trauma, wrote to tell Wiltrout that he was deeply moved at the honor.

The lumber industry faded at the start of the twentieth century, and though Hudson felt the loss, the city was self-sufficient at this point and had lively trade with its sister city Stillwater. Being the county seat, Hudson was guaranteed attention from county and state authorities. In 1913, a toll bridge was built across Lake St. Croix to Stillwater, remaining in place until 1951, when road improvements on both sides of the lake brought about the construction of a modern bridge. Hudson began to attract tourism at a faster pace, and Hudsonites began commuting to Minnesota for employment.

The historic property surveys of the 1970s revealed Hudson to be a treasure chest of significant architecture and sites. The city began a progressive heritage preservation effort and succeeded in putting numerous properties on local and national designation. The town is working to restore its downtown commercial buildings

Sidewheeler ferry *Louis O* operating between Hudson and Lakeland, c1905

and fine old houses. Today, tourism is a priority in this river city, shared in equal part with its role as the gateway to Wisconsin via Interstate 94.

 LOCAL RESOURCES

Hudson Area Chamber of Commerce and Tourism Bureau
502 2nd Street
Hudson, WI 54016
715-386-8411 or 800-657-6775
info@hudsonwi.org
www.hudsonwi.org

Hudson Public Library
911 4th Street
Hudson, WI 54016-1682
715-386-3101
hudsonpl@ifls.lib.wi.us
www.hudsonpubliclibrary.org

Willow River State Park
1034 County Highway A
Hudson, WI 54016
715-386-5931 (office)
715-386-9340 (nature center)
aaron.mason@wisconsin.gov
http://dnr.wi.gov/org/land/parks/specific/willowriver

LODGING OPTIONS

Hudson Area Chamber of Commerce and Tourism Bureau
502 2nd Street
Hudson, WI 54016
715-386-8411 or 800-657-6775
info@hudsonwi.org
www.hudsonwi.org

See also Stillwater for lodging options.

HUDSON TOUR

See map on p. 161.

"NR" indicates National Register properties.

1. BIRKMOSE PARK AND INDIAN BURIAL MOUNDS

The site of a series of large ancient conical burial mounds ranged in a long line high above Lake St. Croix. The park offers picnic facilities and amenities.

2. OLD TOLL BRIDGE ARCH (1936)
1st Street at Walnut Street

The St. Croix Bridge Company built the first interstate toll bridge here in 1913 across Lake St. Croix. The lighted arch was donated in 1936 by Dr. Boyd Williams. The bridge and the arch went dark in 1951 and were replaced by a wider and more modern bridge for auto and truck traffic. The city has restored the arch and a walkway as a welcome to visitors.

3. WILLOW RIVER PIONEER CEMETERY (1850)
Wisconsin Street at 9th Street

Hudson toll bridge, c1917

4. 2ND STREET COMMERCIAL DISTRICT AND OPERA HOUSE BLOCK (1800s, NR)

1st and 2nd streets between Walnut and Locusts streets

The twenty-one-building commercial district in Hudson dates largely from the years after the Civil War, following a devastating fire in 1866.

5. 3RD STREET AND VINE HISTORIC DISTRICT (1800s, NR)

3rd Street between Vine and St. Croix streets

6. WILLIAM PHIPPS HOUSE (1900, NR)/PHIPPS INN

1005 3rd Street

7. JOHN MOFFAT OCTAGON HOUSE AND CARRIAGE HOUSE/ST. CROIX COUNTY HISTORICAL SOCIETY (1855, NR)

1004 3rd Street

Built by Judge John Moffatt in 1855, this building now houses the county historical society. The house is filled with period furnishings, and the Hudson Home and Garden Club has restored the Victorian gardens on the property.

8. ST. CROIX COUNTY COURTHOUSE (1900, NR)

904 3rd Street

9. FREDERICK DARLING HOUSE (1850, NR)

617 3rd Street

10. LEWIS-WILLIAMS HOUSE (1850, NR)

101 3rd Street

11. HUDSON PUBLIC LIBRARY (1900, NR)

3rd Street at Locust Street

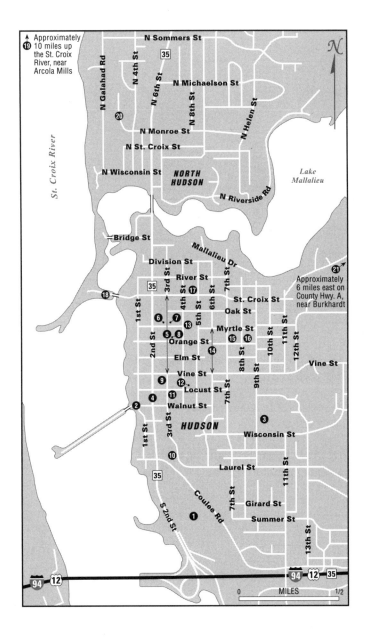

N Sommers St

35

N Galahad Rd

N 4th St

N 6th St

N Michaelson St

N 8th St

N Helen St

19 Approximately 10 miles up the St. Croix River, near Arcola Mills

20

N Monroe St

N St. Croix St

N Wisconsin St

NORTH HUDSON

Lake Mallalieu

N Riverside Rd

St. Croix River

Bridge St

Mallalieu Dr

Division St

River St

3rd St

4th St

5th St

6th St

7th St

St. Croix St

21 Approximately 6 miles east on County Hwy. A, near Burkhardt

18

35

17

Oak St

10th St

11th St

12th St

1st St

2nd St

Orange St

Elm St

6 7 13

5 8

Myrtle St

15 16

8th St

9th St

14

Vine St

Vine St

9

Locust St

12

4

11

Walnut St

7th St

2

1st St

3rd St

HUDSON

3

Wisconsin St

10

35

Laurel St

11th St

1

Coulee Rd

S 2nd St

7th St

Girard St

Summer St

13th St

94 12

94 12 35

0   MILES   1/2

Moffat Octagon House, 1877

12. DR. SAMUEL JOHNSON HOUSE (1900, NR)
405 Locust Street

13. WILLIAM DWELLEY HOUSE (1850, NR)
1002 4th Street

14. 6TH STREET HISTORIC DISTRICT
6th Street between Vine and Myrtle streets

This district includes twelve houses built between 1860 and 1925. Architectural styles range from mid-nineteenth-century Greek Revival through early-twentieth-century Craftsman.

15. SAMUEL MERRIT HOUSE (1900, NR)
904 7th Street

16. HERMAN HUMPHREY HOUSE (1900, NR)
803 Orange Street

17. AUGUST JOHNSON HOUSE (1900, NR)
427 St. Croix Street

18. ST. CROIX STREET CITY LEVEE

19. SOO LINE HIGH BRIDGE (1911, NR)

Bridge design experts have called the Soo Line High (or Arcola) Bridge the most spectacular multispan steel arch bridge in the world. C. A. P. Turner's steel deck railroad bridge soars to 184 feet above Lake St. Croix, anchored on the high bluffs of Wisconsin and Minnesota.

20. CHICAGO, ST. PAUL, MINNEAPOLIS AND OMAHA RAILROAD CAR SHOP HISTORIC DISTRICT (1890–1916, NR)
Roughly bounded by Gallahad Road, Sommers Street, 4th Street North, and St. Croix Street

Thirteen red-brick railroad repair and construction buildings architecturally representative of industrial structures at the turn of the twentieth century.

21. WILLOW RIVER STATE PARK
1034 County Highway A

The historic Willow River, once the site of Hudson's milling industry and earliest settlement, is located five miles east of Hudson at Burkhardt (named for an early mill on the river) and offers 2,891 acres of prairie and forests, the historic millpond, and panoramic river scenery. The most popular hiking trail destinations are the Willow Falls and the scenic overlooks of the river valley. The constant flow of water from the falls and dam account for the abundant wildlife found at the park.

HOULTON AND SOMERSET

HOULTON

Tiny Houlton was named by lumberman Thomas Haggerty from Houlton, Maine, who, with his wife, Elizabeth, came to Stillwater in 1872 and then crossed Lake St. Croix to settle. Haggerty became a mercantile store manager, a tavern and hotel keeper, a farmer, and a property and lumber dealer and served as Houlton's postmaster from 1880 to 1893. Haggerty Street on the town's east end is named for the family and the founder.

The town and the residences built on the bluff overlooking beautiful Lake St. Croix have endured. Houlton is an important gateway from the Stillwater Lift Bridge for those heading north into Wisconsin.

SOMERSET

French Canadian brothers Joseph and Louis Parent came to this area as fur trappers and homesteaders in the late 1840s. The Ojibwe had named the area *Wabizipinikan Zibi* ("Place of the Swan Potato"), which the brothers translated into French as *Pomme de Terre* ("Apple of the Earth," or, in English, "potato"). In time, the brothers' name was very literally translated into English and shortened simply to Apple, and so the river flowing west to Lake St. Croix was named. Many French Canadian families followed the Parent brothers and settled on both sides of the Apple River.

Samuel and Hud Harriman, who had come from Maine to establish a mill and logging company, found the area closest to Lake St. Croix already settled and made their way upstream on the Apple River. They put in a milldam where present-day Main Street crosses the river. They platted the village and named it for their father's hometown in England, built a mercantile store, and started up their lumber mill. When President Lincoln called for volunteers in 1861, Sam enlisted; by 1862, he had earned the rank of general. After the war's end, he returned to Somerset and devoted his energy to developing Harriman's Landing so that travelers and shippers could scale the bluff and travel east to Somerset. Harriman was also a strong force behind bringing the railroad through Somerset and across Lake St. Croix into Minnesota via the now-famous steel arch high bridge.

Though Somerset is now best known for its recreational resources and its role as a gateway to Wisconsin tourism, Somerset French Canadian heritage can still be seen in its churches. The second structure for the

Apple River Falls near Somerset, c1870

Church of St. Anne was commissioned in 1916 by the great E. L. Masqueray, architect of the St. Paul Cathedral as well as the Basilica of St. Mary in Minneapolis.

SOMERSET HISTORIC SITE

Catholic Community of St. Anne
139 Church Hill Road
Somerset, WI 54025
715-247-3310
www.stanne-somerset.org/StAnneSiteNew/
Church_Home.html

 **LOCAL RESOURCES**

Somerset Chamber of Commerce
115 Parent Street
Somerset, WI 54025
715-247-3366
schamber@somtel.net
www.somerset-chamber.com

Village of Somerset
110 Spring Street
PO Box 356 (mailing address)
Somerset, WI 54025
715-247-3395
info@vil.somerset.wi.us
www.vil.somerset.wi.us

See Hudson and Stillwater for lodging options.

DRESSER
AND OSCEOLA

DRESSER

Samuel Dresser donated land to the Soo Line Railroad to build tracks through the town in 1885. The railroad was named Dresser Junction, which was shortened to Dresser in 1940.

Once the train came through in the 1880s, more people came to Dresser to settle. The Canadian Pacific Railway still travels through Dresser for trap rock shipments, and the Osceola and St. Croix Valley Railway also uses the Dresser track for its trains. The first trap rock mine opened in 1914. The historic trap rock building burned in 1993, but mining continues as a viable industry.

DRESSER HISTORIC SITE

**St. Peter's Norwegian Lutheran Church
and Cemetery (1888)**
Estate Street at Church Street

Beautiful and historic white wood-frame church. Drive into the cemetery along the left side of church. Church building retired but still used for special functions. To see the three post-Raphaelite stained-glass windows moved to the new church building or to tour the historic church, call 715-755-2515 or write peace@centurytel.net.

OSCEOLA

Land claims first began in this area in 1844, and a mill company was established by lumbermen from Maine.

They selected a tract that included a creek and high cascade falls that promised sufficient waterpower for a sawmill. The settlement was initially named Leroy, after an unfortunate millhand who was killed in a lumbering accident. Later, James Livingston of the St. Louis Lumber Company in St. Croix Falls chose the name Osceola in honor of a Seminole chieftain. A sawmill was built in 1845 by partners from Taylors Falls, with waterpower provided by Osceola Creek, and named the Osceola Lumber Company. The mill changed hands several times until the Kent brothers came into ownership in 1852. They also built the Cascade Flouring Mill in the same year. A post office opened in 1854 with the name Osceola Mills. A cemetery was established in 1855.

Though little has been written about the Civil War as it affected Osceola, we do know that one of the Maine lumbermen, D. E. Tewksbury, enlisted in Company F, Fourth Wisconsin Regiment, in what turned out to be the last year of the war, 1865. His regiment was posted to the western division of the army for another year. Also, Dr. C. P. Garlick was commissioned assistant surgeon in the Thirty-Fifth Wisconsin Regiment. He contracted a disease while in the service and died in Milwaukee in 1865.

But it is clear that the Civil War years and afterward were busy for the town's commercial development and a time of major growth (and a few losses) for Osceola Mills. The City Mills were built in 1870 by Wilson, Dresser, and Barnes, who sold it to new partners in 1875, who sold it again in 1877. The Osceola Brewery was founded in 1867, and the brewhouse and cellars were steadily expanded over time to permit manufacture and storage of nearly two hundred barrels of beer annually. More mercantile establishments opened for business, and perhaps as a response to the brewery and several very busy town saloons, the ladies of Osceola Mills organized a temperance league in 1874. A boat-building firm succeeded in producing a fair number of steamboats to ply the St. Croix, including the *Dalles,* the *Minnie Will,* the *Nellie Kent,* the *Helen Marr,* and the *Maggie Raney.*

Osceola Mills was stable and economically indepen-dent, and as the timber industry faded after the 1880s, Osceola was in a good position not only to hold onto its population but also to prosper. A good number of the handsome residential structures on the village streets were built after the 1880s, a sign of confidence in the future and sufficient means for the moment.

With the building of a new rail depot for the Soo Line in 1916—and the milling inheritance being firmly of the past—the town shortened its name to Osceola. In 1918, the Cloquet–Moose Lake Fire, started by sparks from a railroad engine that burned rail-side brush, spread as far south as Osceola, and the town lost both commercial and residential buildings.

Today, the entire commercial district is protected with National Register status, and the village streets are filled with nineteenth-century residential architecture. Wilkie Glen and its beautiful twenty-four-foot cascade falls can be reached by a staircase at the south end of town. The Osceola and St. Croix Railway offers scenic tours through many parts of the central St. Croix Val-ley, departing from the historic 1916 Soo Line Osceola Depot. Osceola Landing is one of the most popular boat landings along this stretch of the St. Croix River.

ℹ LOCAL RESOURCES

Village of Osceola
310 Chieftain Street
Osceola, WI 54020
715-294-3498
info@myosceola.com
http://vil.osceola.wi.us
Open Monday thru Friday, 8:00 a.m. to 4:00 p.m.

continues

Osceola Historical Society
408 River Street
Osceola, WI 54020
715-755-2479
barometer@centurytel.net
Open Sundays, June thru October, 2:00 to 4:00 p.m.,
or by appointment.

Osceola Soo Line Depot
114 Depot Road
Osceola, WI 54020
715-755-3570 or 800-711-2590
contact@mtmuseum.org
www.trainride.org

St. Croix ArtBarn
1040 Oak Drive
Osceola, WI 54020
715-294-2787
admin@stcroixartbarn.com
www.stcroixartbarn.com

Village of Dresser and Public Library
102 West Main Street
PO Box 547 (mailing address)
Dresser, WI 54009
715-755-2940
vod@centurytel.net
www.dresserpubliclibrary.org/community.asp
Open Monday thru Friday, 8:00 a.m. to 4:30 p.m.

LODGING OPTIONS

The Valley Motel
211 State Road 35 North
Dresser, WI 54009
715-755-2781 or 800-545-6107
www.thevalleymotel.com

continues

St. Croix River Inn
305 River Street
Osceola, WI 54020
715-294-4248 or 800-645-8820
innkeeper@stcroixriverinn.com

Pleasant Lake Bed and Breakfast
2238 60th Avenue
Osceola, WI 54020
715-294-2545 or 800-294-2545
plakebb@centurytel.net
www.pleasantlake.com

Croixwood on the St. Croix River Bed and Breakfast
421 Ridge Road
Osceola, WI 54020
715-294-2894 or 866-670-3838

Osceola River Valley Inn and Suites
1030 North Cascade Street
PO Box 508 (mailing address)
Osceola, WI 54020
715-294-4060 or 888-791-0022
rivervalley@charterinternet.com
www.osceolarivervalleyinn.com

See also St. Croix Falls and Taylors Falls for lodging options.

OSCEOLA TOUR

See map on p. 173.

"NR" indicates National Register properties.

1. ST. CROIX ARTBARN (1907)
1040 Oak Ridge Drive

Located just west of Osceola. A 103-year-old dairy barn that has been transformed into a community art center.

Cascade Falls, Osceola, c1890

It houses a 180-seat theater and a large gallery hosting artists of local and worldwide recognition.

2. WILKIE GLEN AND CASCADE FALLS
North Cascade Street

3. MILL POND
East of Cascade Street and Wilkie Glen

4. OSCEOLA COMMERCIAL HISTORIC DISTRICT (1874–1950, NR)
North Cascade Street from 1st Avenue to 3rd Avenue

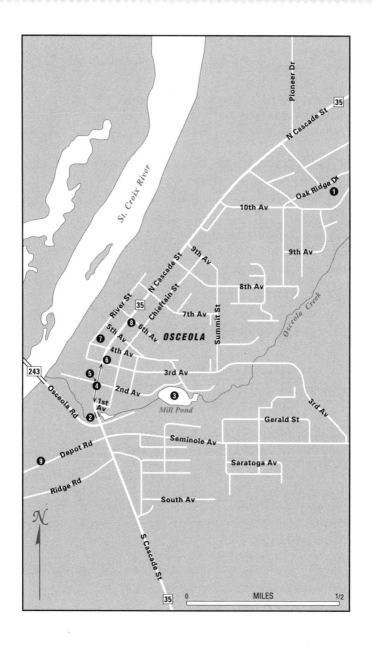

St. Croix River

Pioneer Dr

35

N Cascade St

Oak Ridge Dr

❶

10th Av

9th Av

9th Av

N Cascade St

8th Av

River St

35

Chieftain St

7th Av

Summit St

Osceola Creek

❽ 6th Av

5th Av

OSCEOLA

❼

4th Av

❻

3rd Av

❺

243

❹

2nd Av

❸

1st Av

Mill Pond

Osceola Rd

❷

Gerald St

3rd Av

Depot Rd

Seminole Av

❾

Saratoga Av

Ridge Rd

N

South Av

S Cascade St

35

0   MILES   1/2

5. OLD POLK COUNTY COURTHOUSE / GEIGER BUILDING (1875, NR)

201 North Cascade Street

6. FIRST BAPTIST CHURCH / CORNERSTONE SQUARE (1910, NR)

201 3rd Avenue

7. EMILY OLSON HOUSE (1862) / OSCEOLA HISTORICAL SOCIETY

408 River Street

The Emily Olson House has served as a home and library and is now the headquarters of the Osceola Historical Society. The dining room, living room, and one upstairs bedroom are furnished to represent its earlier history. Other rooms serve as work rooms and archive storage for the society.

8. ALVAH HEALD HOUSE (1875, NR)

202 6th Avenue

Alvah Heald was born in Temple, New Hampshire, in 1832 and in 1864 enlisted as a lieutenant in Company E, Sixth New Hampshire Regiment.

9. MINNEAPOLIS, ST. PAUL AND SAULT (SOO) SAINT MARIE RAILWAY DEPOT (1916, NR)

114 Depot Road

This restored brick depot is the home of the Osceola and St. Croix Valley Railway. The Soo Line did not customarily build such an opulent depot in small towns, but a prominent Osceola businessman persuaded the railroad to provide the town with this handsome design. Gift shop, railroad displays. Tickets for train rides sold here. Open weekends May thru October.

ST. CROIX FALLS

The village of St. Croix Falls, just across from Taylors Falls on the Dalles of the St. Croix River, was happily situated above a source of substantial waterpower, a falls the Ojibwe named *Menominikeshi Kakabikang* ("The Falls of the Ricebird River"). In its early years, the site was known to traders and lumbermen as the Falls of St. Croix.

The first claim on the east bank of the St. Croix River was made by an Illinois lumber company in 1839. The company included Franklin Steele, who was already the principal owner of mills at the village of St. Anthony on the Mississippi River. Steele had come upriver aboard a birch-bark canoe in the summer of 1838, with eight men laboring to keep the craft moving steadily against the current.

Steele sold out his share to William Hungerford in 1842 and went downriver to settle at Stillwater. Hungerford then sold the mill in 1845 to James Perrington. Perrington found the mill in considerable need of repair. A visitor to the falls, Caleb Cushing, was persuaded to invest the needed cash to bring the mill into operation again. Together Perrington and Cushing formed the Boston Lumber Company. Three years later the mill burned down. Cushing stayed on in the area, and Perrington moved down the St. Croix to the Willow River to open another milling operation.

Franklin Steele returned to St. Croix Falls in 1847, built a dam across the east channel of the river, and commissioned a new sawmill that opened for business in 1848. A joint stock company of local men, grandly known as the St. Croix Manufacturing and Improvement Company (SCM&IC), was established to lay out a new town, with Caleb Cushing acting as land agent. From that time forward the land and the company were under constant legal dispute, lasting well into the 1860s, while other lumbermen came to build mills at the falls.

The company managed to build a hotel for the millhands and lumbermen, called Cushing House. A flouring mill and warehouses were also installed on the landing, as were many houses, stores, and a schoolhouse. Other settlers made their contributions with new stores, workshops, and a second hotel, the St. Croix House.

With the death of the principal SCM&IC officers, the entire town plan was cut adrift. Though the new mill continued to be run during the summer months, the hotel was abandoned, and, as one visitor noted on passing through, "the basement of the great hotel is a summer resort for cattle as a shelter from the sun." The mill burned down in 1864.

The years following the Civil War showed the ever-present hope of the pioneer entrepreneur. One corporation followed another—the Chisago Mining and Manufacturing Company, the Great European and American Land Company—in attempts to jump-start a viable town with an industrial base to support it.

St. Croix Falls quietly settled into a residential and commercial district on the river with a steamboat landing site and enough mercantile trade and skilled craftsmen to keep change in the family pockets. Two new mills, one for flouring and one for lumber, were built in the 1870s and ran successfully, though at modest output, enough for the local community's needs.

The boom years for St. Croix River lumbering, the 1880s, provided a high industrial tide for St. Croix Falls, though the decade started out with the loss of the old Cushing Hotel to fire in 1882, erasing a long-standing town landmark and offsetting somewhat sadly Cushing's commission of a new land office building in the same year. As lumbering faded by the end of the century, St. Croix Falls had stabilized as a small but attractive town with a large wagon manufacturing concern, a significant furniture company, and an extensive leather and harness firm that supplied the two sizeable local stables, which, together, had fifty-five horses and therefore also

St. Croix Falls view from the north, c1880

required numerous blacksmiths and farriers. Grocers, mercantiles, some saloons, and several professional offices—physicians, lawyers, dentists, pharmacists—made St. Croix Falls a self-sufficient community.

St. Croix Falls' rapids had not done well for its mill owners. Nevertheless, it was a landmark of great beauty, giving a name to the towns on either side of the St. Croix. In 1906, the Minneapolis General Electric Company undertook to build a power dam at the falls and, finally resolving a half century of property owner-ship battles, secured the land titles and the water rights to bring the project into being. Suddenly, the little town that just couldn't find an identity, did.

The Minneapolis General Electric Company was an interesting animal, one with many skins. Under the company name were two new corporations, the St. Croix Falls Wisconsin Improvement Company and the St. Croix Falls Minnesota Improvement Company. These corporations were the actual owners of the acquired property and water rights. Underneath these corpora-tions were the holdings of the Weyerhaeuser Company, which by this time had acquired Isaac Staples's St. Croix River Navigation and Improvement Company, which had in turn built the St. Croix boom site at Stillwater, and the St. Croix Lumbermen's Dam and Boom Company, known locally as the Nevers Dam, which had been constructed upriver in the late 1840s to help manage timber rafting. The Nevers Dam, once under the Minneapolis General Electric Company's control, was shut down in preparation to break ground on the riverbed.

Construction of the dam began in 1904, and the new power dam went into operation in 1906, with high-tension power lines bringing electricity to Minneapolis. With the completion of the dam, the beautiful rapids were gone forever.

But St. Croix Falls, despite the loss of the irreplaceable rapids, did very well with the power project. Engineers, contractors, supervisors, machinists, bulldozer

St. Croix Falls Hydroelectric Dam, 1923

drivers, crane operators, boiler men, blasters, welders, electricians, and laborers all needed supplies and housing during the project. A dynamo was set up to provide power for light, permitting night work. A blacksmith shop ran three forges for the construction workers who were using horse teams to move out material.

A crew had been sent upriver to strengthen and repair the Nevers Dam and begin to clear the land for the flowage that would be created by the massive buildup of water from the new power dam downriver. The town of Wolf Creek, near the Nevers Dam, lost its riverside thoroughfare, but a new road was constructed inland for the town.

Some three hundred men were employed on the construction site at any one time, working seven days a week, morning or night shifts. Many new immigrants were grateful for the employment, and the *St. Croix*

Valley Standard reported that there was a camp of Austrians living in barracks on the river flats, many with their families. There was also a Mexican camp. Men slept in boardinghouses, rented rooms, hotel storage closets, and civic building attics. The *Standard* interviewed resident Henry Lee, who reported that "these fellows were tougher than a boiled owl. They'd swim in the icy water, sleep in cold shacks." Lee went on to describe the one constant coming out of every company cook's shanty—spaghetti. It was cheap and filling. When not on the project site, many of these new immigrants would play instruments, sing, or dance. In the city cemetery, more than a few gravestones with European and Hispanic names reflect the nationalities of the men who died on the dam site.

As the chutes of the completed dam were finally closed, people came from great distances to watch the flowage fill. It widened to three times its original breadth, covering the old river roads and many upstream islands. Professionals working on dams came from around the world to view and tour the finished dam, including engineers from Russia.

After the dam went online in January 1907, company ownership went through changes, and in 1912 the Consumers Power Company (CPC) acquired the Minneapolis General Electric Company and its subsidiaries. The CPC was succeeded by the Northern State Power Company, which had formed in 1916. The St. Croix Hydroelectric Dam has been humming along ever since.

At last, the town that had not been able to realize an industrial success from its waterpower came into its own. Many who live in St. Croix Falls have their livelihoods tied to the operation of the dam or are the children of those who once did.

Today, St. Croix Falls has reinvented itself as many of the other St. Croix Valley cities have done, working to support tourism and the enjoyment of the great beauty of the river and the historic community above the great power dam where a waterfall once flowed.

ℹ️ LOCAL RESOURCES

City of St. Croix Falls
710 Highway 35 South
St. Croix Falls, WI 54024
715-483-3929
www.cityofstcroixfalls.com

Falls Chamber of Commerce/
St. Croix Falls Historical Society
106 South Washington Street
St. Croix Falls, WI 54024
715-483-3580
director@fallschamber.org
www.fallschamber.org

St. Croix Valley Group Tours
651-451-6315 or 800-447-4958
tour@scfwi.com
www.scfwi.com/gto.htm

St. Croix Falls Public Library
210 North Washington Street
St. Croix Falls, WI 54024
715-483-1777
scflibrary@ifls.lib.wi.us
www.stcroixfallslibrary.org

Interstate State Park/Wisconsin
State Highway 35
PO Box 703
St. Croix Falls, WI 54024
715-483-3747
www.dnr.state.wi.us/org/LAND/parks/specific/interstate

🛏️ LODGING OPTIONS

Holiday Inn Express St. Croix Valley
2190 Highway 8
St. Croix Falls, WI 54024
715-483-5775 or 888-465-4329
www.hiexpress.com

continues

Dalles House Motel
726 Highway 35
St. Croix Falls, WI 54024
715-483-3206 or 888-725-6913
dalleshousemotel@charterinternet.com

Wissahickon Farms Country Inn Bed and Breakfast
2263 Maple Drive
St. Croix Falls, WI 54024
715-483-3986
stay@wissainn.com
www.wissainn.com

See also Taylors Falls, Dresser, and Osceola for lodging options.

ST. CROIX FALLS TOUR

See map on p. 183.

"NR" indicates National Register properties.

1. INTERSTATE STATE PARK/WISCONSIN (1938)
South of Highway 8, east side of bridge

Interstate State Park, which lies on both sides of the St. Croix River, is Wisconsin's oldest state park and has the greatest percentage of its parklands, as well as river views of the spectacular Wisconsin Dalles.

2. THOMAS THOMPSON HOUSE (C. 1890, NR)
205 South Adams Street

Home of the first man on the crew of the St. Croix Falls Hydroelectric Dam project lost to accidental death, in 1905.

3. CUSHING LAND AGENCY BUILDING (1882, NR)
106 South Washington Street

Now the site of the Falls Chamber of Commerce and the St. Croix Falls Historical Society.

4. ST. CROIX FALLS AUDITORIUM / FESTIVAL THEATRE (1918, NR)
201 North Washington Street

5. RIVER SPIRIT SCENIC OVERLOOK
North Washington Street (river side) between Louisiana and Maryland streets

A handsome public overlook above the St. Croix Hydro-electric Dam. Overlook plaza features a commissioned sculpture, *River Spirit,* a 1,300-pound millstone from the now-vanished Thompson-Boughton Mill, and a historic marker on the development of waterpower and milling.

6. ST. CROIX HYDROELECTRIC DAM AND POWERHOUSE

7. LAMAR COMMUNITY CENTER (1900, NR)
1488 200th Street

A rural two-room schoolhouse on the eastern edge of St. Croix Falls. Site of summer arts camp for children and annual Lamar Music Festival in August, www.lamarcommunity.org.

8. ST. CROIX NATIONAL SCENIC RIVERWAY VISITOR CENTER, NATIONAL PARK SERVICE
401 North Hamilton Street

One of three National Park Service interpretive and information centers for visitors to the St. Croix National Scenic Riverway.

9. LIONS PARK
Highway 87

A riverside park with playground, picnic shelter, boat landing, and a small brook that empties into the river. A historic marker reads, "Site of a 1770 historic battle between three tribes—Ojibwe, Dakota and Fox. Ojibwe victorious, few remaining Fox joined the Sac tribe."

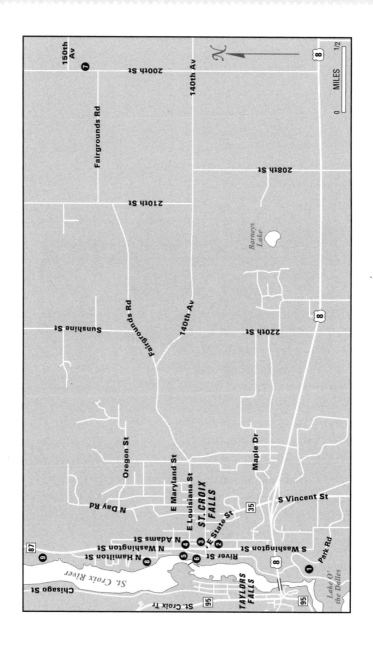

Blueberry pickers crossing the St. Croix River, 1910

THE WILD RIVER

The districts of Minnesota and Wisconsin north of the twins—Taylors Falls and St. Croix Falls—are truly the Wild River regions. Here the old government roads run on their original courses, and the towns that waxed and waned along those roads and railroad routes are still pinned to the map with some fine old buildings, historic cemeteries, and pride in their inheritance.

Here also are some of the best of the Minnesota and Wisconsin state parks, county forests and state wildlife areas, restored forts and trading posts, and the home of the St. Croix Band of Ojibwe.

There are few opportunities to cross the river above the twin towns: once at U.S. Highway 70 connecting Minnesota's Interstate 35 to Wisconsin's gateway city of Grantsburg and again at County Road 48 at the very top of the St. Croix before it crosses at last into Danbury, Wisconsin, and meets Highway 35 on its journey to Superior.

Where Highway 35 heads north and leaves the St. Croix River's flow to the northeast, we find the historic confluence of the St. Croix and the Namekagon (in Ojibwe, *Namekagon Zibi,* or Sturgeon River), and the St. Croix continues north and east to its naturally dammed great flowage (*Namekawagon,* or the Sturgeon Dam), the historic portage to the Brule River and its passage up to Lake Superior. This was the historic trading route for the Ojibwe, the French and English fur traders, the missionaries, and the explorers.

It is a vast area of greatly varied terrain and land usage: farms carved out of forests, forests allowed to return to nature, open prairie, bogs and marshes.

Much—most—of the St. Croix is inaccessible by road above the twin towns; now only hikers, campers, and those using water transportation (with skill and training) will reach the shoreline. If traveling by land vehicle, you will want a DeLorme atlas (the latest for both Minnesota and Wisconsin), purchasable at any major bookseller and very frequently at highway-side convenience and fuel stores. A general highway map, excellent as such can be for long-distance travel, *will not* sketch for you the small, ever-shifting country roads that fill the Wild River townships. Nor are USGS topographic quad maps recommended for Wild River land vehicle travel: use them for hiking and camping in state parks.

But those who were here long before the Europeans—the St. Croix Band of Ojibwe—and those who passed through more recently—the French and English traders, the loggers and miners, the countless immigrants, the road builders, and the rail layers—left behind much of their culture and way of life, and these markers are still there to be found.

This final chapter will highlight many of those historic sites and unique locales and bring travelers to communities that maintain a distinctive lifestyle.

Gordon Tote Bridge, north of Gordon, Wisconsin, c1890s

MINNESOTA

CHISAGO COUNTY ROAD 16 AND WILD RIVER STATE PARK

Leave Taylors Falls by taking Highway 95 along the main business thoroughfare, and turn right onto Chicago Street. Chicago Street will become Chisago County Road 16 and hug the river line on the bluffs until finally turning due west (Wild Mountain Water Park will be on your left at the curve). You are now running the southern boundary of Wild River State Park in Amador Township. Take a right at Reed Avenue (Chisago County Road 71) until you reach Park Trail (County Road Trail). Turn right into the park.

The park contains the sites of both the Connors Goose Creek Post and the Samuel Fur Post; traces of the 1850s Point Douglas–Superior government road (on the National Register); and archaeological sites tied to 6,000 years of Native American life, including Dakota, Ojibwe, Sauk, and Meskwaki. Two townsites were platted with the present park boundaries by lumbermen from

Nevers Dam from Wisconsin shore, 1897

Sweden and New England. The Nevers Dam Overlook permits a view of the river where the first dam to control the passage of logs downriver was constructed. The visitor center offers historical and cultural exhibits, and many of the park trails have interpretive signage of the historic sites found within Wild River State Park.

RIVER ROAD TO ALMELÜND

Leave Wild River State Park on Park Trail, cross over Reed Avenue (Chisago County Road 71), and take Park Trail (Chisago County Road 12) into Almelünd ("elm grove" in Swedish). Most of the settlers were from Småland. The town was known as Church Hill until the Swedish community was awarded a post office in 1887. John Almquist ("elm twig or branch") was the first postmaster, and the community wished to honor him. There is a fine small museum in the old schoolhouse as well as a pioneer cabin, both in the park on Highway 95. The Almelünd Cemetery dating from 1887 is adjacent to Immanuel Lutheran Church just as you enter the town.

Old Government Road, Taylors Falls to Almelund, c1880

RIVER ROAD TO SUNRISE FERRY

Return up Park Trail to Wild River State Park, turn north up Reed Avenue (Chisago County Road 71), and take the sharp left turn at the top of the road. Follow River Road into Sunrise. The remaining buildings from this once bustling logging and milling town are the old bank, the 1861 schoolhouse, and the lovely 1862 Sunrise Cemetery on Sunrise Ferry Road with its many Civil War burials, considered one of the most beautiful cemeteries in the state. The tall pines were planted at the time of European settlement. The Sunrise River (in Ojibwe, *Memokage Zibi,* or Keep Sunrising River) flows through the town and down to the St. Croix. The Sunrise Ferry Road drops to the St. Croix, where, on exactly the opposite bank, it meets the Wisconsin landing at the site of the now-vanished village of Evergreen.

SUNRISE ROAD TO RUSH FERRY

Take Sunrise Road (County Road 9) north to Peaceful Valley Road and turn north. You are now on a stretch of the old Point Douglas–Superior government road. You are in Rusheba Township, a name formed out of the word *rush* in the name Rush River (in Ojibwe, *Ga-Shashaganushko-kani Zibi,* or Place of Rushes River), which flows east here down to the St. Croix. Bulrushes are abundant in the shallows of lakes and rivers and were commonly used by Native Americans for weaving into mats.

When you cross 460th Street, the road becomes County Road 57. Just before you reach Ferry Road, you will see the 1871 Taylor Cemetery on your left. A cousin of Ulysses S. Grant is buried here.

Take the right turn on Ferry Road, and follow it east toward the St. Croix. When you have crossed River Road, you are in the Chengwatana (from the Ojibwe, *jin-wak odena,* or pine city) State Forest. At the river shore, where Ferry Road comes down to the old landing, you are directly opposite the landing on the Wisconsin shore for the now-vanished village of Randall.

FERRY ROAD TO RUSH CITY

Take Ferry Road (County Road 5) west into Rush City, a town settled by Irish, New Englanders, and, later, Swedes. The crossroads village on the Rush River was the site of a large trading post, later a hotel, store, lumberyard, and railroad depot (1869). George Folsom settled here, and his house was a popular stopover for travelers on the government road, including Folsom's friend General William Tecumseh Sherman. The Grant House (1896, NR) at 4th and Bremer was built to serve the railroad community. The J. C. Carlson House (1899, NR) at 6th and Bremer is a massive Queen Anne frame residence designed by architect Augustus F. Gauger (who gained fame for his similar houses for the wealthy built on St. Paul's Dayton's Bluff) for the Rush City bank president and civic leader.

Rush City had developed a potato farming industry and was shipping potatoes by rail from eleven ware-

Original Grant House Hotel, Rush City, c1881

houses by 1870. A spur line was built across the river into Grantsburg, where a turntable would permit the small engine to realign for the run back to Rush City. The train was much faster and more convenient than the ferry for all the people who wanted to pick blueberries on the Wisconsin side of the St. Croix. Blueberry Trail, a half mile north of Ferry Road, also runs toward the river on the old rail bed and stops where the bridge ended on the Minnesota side.

To continue on the Minnesota side, drive north from Rush City on Highway 361 to Highway 70, turn east, and take the last left turn before the river bridge to park at the Marshland Environmental Education Center of the St. Croix National Scenic Riverway. The center provides educational programs and river orientations for groups of ten or more during the summer months by reservation or by appointment. See p. 201 for contact info.

To move on into Wisconsin, drive north from Rush City on Highway 361 to Highway 70, turn east, and drive over the St. Croix River for tours north, east, or south. See p. 195 and following.

Construction of the Twin City & Lake Superior Railway through Pine County, 1907

THE NORTH WEST COMPANY FUR POST (1804, NR) AND PINE CITY FERRY

Take Forest Boulevard (Highway 361) north into Pine City; alternatively, take Interstate 35 north and exit at Highway 324 (Pine City). Drive west over Interstate 35 and take Pokegama Lake Road (County Road 7), cross over a small tributary into Pokegama Lake, and take the next left to reach the historic site's entrance.

The North West Company Fur Post is a reconstructed winter trading post (open only from late spring to early autumn) with log living quarters surrounding the stockade. Built by the company as a winter depot for its trapper-traders, the site is open as a reenactment experience at an Ojibwe encampment and fur trading post and managed by the Minnesota Historical Society.

To reach the Pine City Ferry landing, which connected the Minnesota community to the Wisconsin shore below Grantsburg, head east out of Pine City on County Road 8, which becomes St. Croix Road (County Road 118). When the Snake River appears on your left, you have entered the Chengwatana State Forest (from the Ojibwe, *jinwak odena,* "pine city"). Stay on this road through the Snake River Campground until it turns sharply to the left and drops down to the river bank. Immediately across on the Wisconsin side of the river is Ferry Road, which leads up the bluff to Grantsburg (see p. 197).

CHENGWATANA STATE FOREST AND ST. CROIX STATE PARK (1936, NR)

The Chengwatana State Forest terrain consists of forested upland islands surrounded by marsh and brush. Three rivers, the Kettle, Snake, and St. Croix, flow through the forest.

St. Croix State Park lies to the northeast of Pine City, where the marshy terrain is ideal for cranberry bogs but very soggy for supporting modern roads. So head north on Interstate 35 to Highway 48 (Hinckley exit) and then east across the Kettle River, and drive two to three miles to the park entrance at St. Croix Park Road (County Road 22).

The St. Croix State Park, originally developed as the St. Croix Recreational Demonstration Area by the National Park Service in the 1930s, is Minnesota's largest state park. This 33,895-acre marshland is fed by tributaries to the Kettle River (in Ojibwe, *Akiko Zibi),* named for the water-worn rocks of the lower river that are now carved out deeply enough to retain water. The Kettle has been designated as a state wild and scenic river.

As many as 164 structures built by the Civilian Conservation Corps and the Works Progress Administration survive in that program's classic rustic log and stone architecture; it's the largest collection of New Deal projects in Minnesota. The entire historic district was listed as a National Historic Landmark in 1997.

Travelers should exit back up onto Highway 48. Return west to reach Hinckley to take Interstate 35 south, or head east to cross the St. Croix River to reach Danbury, Wisconsin. Travelers can take Wisconsin Highway 35 to points south and southwest.

WISCONSIN

THE ST. CROIX BAND OF OJIBWE

At Danbury, we enter the world of the St. Croix Band of Ojibwe, who have been in the northwestern area of present-day Wisconsin for over six hundred years, eventually moving southward from Lake Superior to "the place where there is food upon the waters," referring to the great availability of wild rice. The Ojibwe named the headwaters of the St. Croix River *Manoominikeshiinyagziibi,* or Rail Ricing River.

Excluded from the 1854 Treaty of La Pointe, the St. Croix Ojibwe found themselves as a nonrecognized Ojibwe tribal community. Though pressured to relocate to a tribal reservation to secure annuities, most of the St. Croix Band remained in the St. Croix Valley. After a long period of discord and broken promises, the St. Croix

Ojibwe people outside of church, Danbury, c1910

Band in Wisconsin regained full federal recognition in 1854 under the name St. Croix Ojibwe Indians of Wisconsin. The tribal offices are in Webster and two very successful casinos are located in Danbury and Turtle Lake.

The St. Croix Ojibwe Reservation in Wisconsin is not one large block of land but rather scattered villages—Danbury, Bashaw Lake, Big Sand Lake, Clam Lake, Big Round Lake, Hertel, and others—spread across four counties: Burnett, Barron, Polk, and Washington. The St. Croix and Yellow Rivers flow through the reservation villages, and many lakes are also found in the region. The communities gather every year in late August for the Annual St. Croix Wild Rice Pow-Wow, a three-day celebration at the tribal center in Hertel that hosts drummers and singers from all over the United States.

FORTS FOLLE AVOINE (1802, NR)

From Danbury, drive south on Highway 35 to County Road U, and turn right to drive through Yellow Lake. The forts will be on your right just after you cross a small channel of Little Yellow Lake.

This re-created trading post (pronounced *fort foll avwahn*) is a living history site located on eighty acres of wooded land along the Yellow River, in the midst of the communities of the St. Croix Band of Ojibwe. The park is a National Register site housing the Burnett County Historical Society.

Visitors can rendezvous with voyageurs, observe Ojibwe artists working on traditional crafts, and be guided by interpreters dressed in the native and European clothing of two hundred years ago. The park offers a museum, a theater, and a book and gift store. The Palmer House Research Library is heavily used. Large crafts such as quilts are on exhibit in the 1887 Karlsborg one-room school. The Great Folle Avoine Fur Trade Rendezvous takes place the fourth weekend of July every year.

Northern Pacific spur line from Rush City into Grantsburg, 1951

GRANTSBURG

It is hard to think of Grantsburg, today the gateway to so much of Wisconsin's recreational and environmental regions, as the terminus of a short-line railroad carried over the St. Croix from Rush City. But that little rail line did indeed exist, complete with depot and roundtable to turn the little engine around to return over the river. What were people traveling for? Blueberries!

The town is filled with lovely nineteenth-century buildings and has some handsome city parks. Several of the historic buildings have been honored with plaques by the Grantsburg Area Historical Society. There are two National Register structures in town: the Burnett County Abstract Company Building at 214 Oak Street (1900) and the Jacobson House and Mill Site (1850) east of town on County Road M. The Grantsburg Public Library has a local history room that is heavily used and open during library hours.

Burnett County Courthouse, Grantsburg, c1880

CREX MEADOWS

Crex Meadows is the largest wildlife area in Wisconsin, home of more than 270 species of birds and other wildlife amid 30,000 acres of prairie, wetlands, and forests. Crex Meadows is renowned for the migrating sandhill cranes that bring the public and the media every spring to watch the environmentalists work to foster this currently endangered species. Crex is host to over 100,000 people every year at the visitor center, observation areas, picnic and rest area, and trails. An open house to say good-bye to the migrating birds takes place the second weekend in October. Crex is fully accessible and permits tours through the preserve by car.

RUSTIC ROAD 15, FISH LAKE ROAD, LIND, BENSON, AND EVERGREEN

Take South Pine Street (County Road 87) south out of Grantsburg, and turn right on Fish Lake Road. You are now traveling Wisconsin's Rustic Road No. 15, one of many unspoiled roads in the state that have been recognized for remaining virtually unchanged from the early years of European settlement. Notice along your right the high, flat embankment running parallel to the road: this was the rail bed of the line that ran between Grantsburg and Rush City. At the first curve to the south, you are passing through the lost town of Lind.

As Fish Lake Road curves farther south and becomes West River Road, watch on the left, just past Pleasant Prairie Road, for the tiny but nicely preserved Benson family cemetery, surrounded by its original iron picket fencing and with just one burial, Swen Johan Bengtson, 1849–1918. This was the location of the town of Benson, which has disappeared. Swen built a store here, which served as post office, depot, and snack shop for train passengers.

West River Road runs due south through wooded land. You have been traveling for some time through the Governor Knowles State Forest, which stretches for more than fifty miles along the east bank of the St. Croix River. Soon, you will see signs that you are passing through the Burnett County Forest.

Take the left turn onto Evergreen from the West River Road. Just after passing 300th Street, the old Evergreen School, the last remnant of the town, will be on the hillside on your left where the Trade River (in Ojibwe, *Otawa Zibi,* or Trader River) comes down to the St. Croix. A further treasure awaits you at 330th and Evergreen: the Sterling Swedish Lutheran Chapel (1870s) and Cemetery. Stop, park, walk into the building, sign the register. See how tiny the space is, admire the handmade wooden backless benches and the glass window allowing light to pour in through the greenery beyond. Walk the very old pioneer cemetery.

Follow Evergreen Road to its reconnection with River Road, and turn south to a town that was once named Sterling and is now called Wolf Creek.

WOLF CREEK

Wolf Creek is a village that takes its name from the stream (Ojibwe name unknown) that passes through the village and down to the river. The Wolf Creek School, 1892–1958, still has its bell in the cupola and serves today as a church. The Wolf Creek Cemetery is adjacent to the building. Just as River Road makes a slight jog, note the classic old cabin resort next to Riverside Auto. How many such cabin courts there must have once been along the St. Croix! Continue south on River Road to the Nevers Dam Wayside.

NEVERS DAM (1889–1954)

Also known as the St. Croix River Dam, the Nevers was the largest wooden dam in the world, and the Bear Trap Gate—a massive eighty feet wide—the largest dam gate.

The Nevers Dam was named for Charlie Nevers, a farmer from whom Frederick Weyerhaeuser bought the shoreline property to build a dam eleven miles above St. Croix Falls. Logs were getting jammed up at Angle Rock, and the frustration and complication of sorting them out gave rise to a need to control the water's flow and the logs' passage in some kind of orderly fashion. The cost was an enormous $250,000, the investors hoping that they would recoup their investments by charging tolls for every branded log that passed through the Bear Trap Gate and by an improvement in the operations down at the St. Croix boom site.

The dam was run on a two-week cycle: the sluice gates would be closed, and water would back up behind the dam. The lumbermen upstream had just under twelve days to float their logs into the water. The gates would then be raised, and the logs would be passed through the Bear Gate in a controlled fashion and ride a wave of high water down toward the mills at Stillwater.

As logging faded away after 1900, the Nevers Dam was sold to Northern States Power to permit control of water while building the St. Croix Hydroelectric Dam downstream at St. Croix Falls. That power dam was finished, and there seemed no reason to deal with the enormous Nevers Dam until heavy rains and extremely high water in the spring of 1954 undermined its footings. Most of the structure was removed. With its disappearance, locals also lost a handy way to drive across the river, the top of the dam being perfectly flat.

As you stand at the landing of the Nevers Dam site, know that a 100-foot section of the dike remains in place underwater on the Wisconsin side.

Continue down the River Road along the shoreline to enter the north neighborhoods of St. Croix Falls.

ℹ️ LOCAL RESOURCES

Wild River State Park
39797 Park Trail
Center City, MN 55012
651-583-2125
651-583-2925 (park naturalist)
www.dnr.state.mn.us/state_parks/wild_river

Marshland Center of the St. Croix National Scenic Riverway
15975 Highway 70
Pine City, MN
320-629-2148
Open to the public by appointment.

Rush City Chamber of Commerce
PO Box 713
Rush City, MN 55069
320-358-4639
director@rushcitychamber.com
www.rushcitychamber.com

North West Company Fur Post
12551 Voyageur Lane
Pine City, MN 55063
320-629-6356
nwfurpost@mnhs.org
www.mnhs.org/nwcfurpost

continues

Open Memorial Day thru Labor Day, Monday and Thursday thru Saturday, 10:00 a.m. to 5:00 p.m., Sundays noon to 5:00 p.m. Open holidays. School and group tours by appointment.

Pine City Chamber of Commerce
900 4th Street Southeast
Suite 85
Pine City, MN 55063
320-6629-4565
www.pinecitychamber.com

Chengwatana State Forest and Snake River Campground
651-583-2125
www.dnr.state.mn.us/state_forests/sft00012

St. Croix State Park
30065 St. Croix Park Road
Hinckley, MN 55037
320-384-6591
www.dnr.state.mn.us/state_parks/st_croix

St. Croix Band of Ojibwe
St. Croix Tribal Center
24663 Angeline Ave
Webster, WI 54893
800-236-2195
www.stcciw.com

Forts Folle Avoine Historical Park/Burnett County Historical Society
8500 County Road U
Danbury, WI 54830
715-866-8890
www.theforts.org
Open Memorial Day thru Labor Day, Wednesday thru Saturday, 10:00 a.m. to 4:00 p.m., Sunday 11:00 a.m. to 4:00 p.m.

Burnett County Chamber
7410 County Road K
Siren, WI 54872
www.burnettcounty.com

continues

Grantsburg Village Office and Chamber
316 South Brad Street
Grantsburg, WI 54840
715-463-2405
villageoffice@grantsburgwi.com
www.grantsburgwi.com

Grantsburg Area Historical Society
133 West Wisconsin Avenue
Grantsburg, WI 54840
715-689-2374
Open Memorial Day thru Labor Day, Sunday 1:00 to 4:00 p.m.,
or by appointment.

Grantsburg Public Library
416 South Pine Street
Grantsburg, WI 54840–4404
715-463-2244
www.grantsburgwi.com/library.htm

Crex Meadows
102 East Crex Avenue
Grantsburg, WI 54840–7400
715-463-2896
www.crexmeadows.org

Wild River Outfitters
15177 State Road 70
Grantsburg, WI 54840–8509
www.wildriverpaddling.com
Canoe, kayak rental, and shuttle services.

Pardun's Canoe Rental and Shuttle Service
Main Street and 4th Avenue South
Danbury, WI
715-656-7881
www.pardunscanoerental.com

Eric's Canoe Rental and Shuttle Service
Wild River State Park
Highway 12
651-270-1561
www.ericscanoerental.com

🛏 LODGING OPTIONS

Grant House Hotel and Eatery
80 East 4th Street
Rush City, MN 55069–9035
320-358-3661

AmericInn North Branch
38675 14th Avenue (Interstate 35 at Highway 95)
North Branch, MN 55056
651-674-3267 (local) or 800-494-0562 (national)
www.americinn-northbranch.com

Budget Host Inn and Suites of North Branch
6010 Main Street
North Branch, MN 55056
651-277-8000 (local) or 800-283-4678 (national)
budgethost_nb@yahoo.com
budgethostnorthbranch.com

Old Oak Inn
920 Main Street South
Pine City, MN 55063
800-524-2512
oldoakinn@mywdo.com
www.oldoakinn.net

Days Inn Hinckley
104 Grindstone Court (Interstate 35 at Hinckley Exit)
PO Box 337 (mailing address)
Hinckley, MN 55037
320-384-7751
generalmanager04267@wynhg.com
www.daysinn.com

Smoland Prairie Homestead Inn
11658 State Highway 70
Grantsburg, WI 54840
715-689-2528
smolandinn@smolandinn.com
www.smolandinn.com

Cedar Point Resort
12480 Cedar Point Lane
Grantsburg, WI 54840
715-488-2224
www.cedarpointresort.us

ACKNOWLEDGMENTS

This book is the result of sound advice, referrals to resources, and generous access to information offered by the Minnesota and Wisconsin historical societies, their state historic preservation offices, and the many county and local historical societies that exist on both sides of the St. Croix River.

First, thanks must go to Brent Peterson, director and curator of the Washington County Historical Society, who, knowing the great complexity of that county's story and the size and number of the St. Croix communities I needed to document, never failed in generosity, great connections, sheer breadth of knowledge, and unwavering cheerfulness and courtesy.

The county historical societies provided the much-needed big picture, and the local historical societies, the fine details, up and down the river. The librarians at the St. Croix Collection of the Stillwater Public Library gave me a great deal of their time and access to invaluable materials and publications.

After the reading, a researcher must go out the door and travel far afield. In this way, wonderful sites are found, lovely people met, and many questions answered. There were more than a few "aha!" and "wow!" moments on the road, and I traveled in the most glorious scenery in the country. Could I have been more blessed?

Of course my thanks must go to family and friends who, after ten books written, have refined their affectionate art of waiting patiently through the final months of steady writing, fact-checking, writing, revisiting sites, writing, more reading, paring down a massive manuscript to publishable size, and then writing, around the clock. You know who you are, and you know how I feel. I thank you most wholeheartedly.

The author takes responsibility for all information offered in this book. Any mistakes are my own, and your corrections are welcomed.

FURTHER READING

Ahlgren, Dorothy Eaton and Mary Beeler. *A History of Prescott, Wisconsin: A River City and Farming Community on the St. Croix and Mississippi*. Prescott, WI: Prescott Area Historical Society, 1996.

Benson, David R. *Stories in Log and Stone: The Legacy of the New Deal in Minnesota State Parks*. St. Paul: Minnesota Department of Natural Resources, 2002.

Breining, Greg and Linda Watson. *Gathering of Waters: A Guide to Minnesota's Rivers*. St. Paul: Minnesota Department of Natural Resources, 1977.

Buck, Anita Albrecht. *Steamboats on the St. Croix*. St. Cloud, MN: North Star Press, 1990.

Carley, Kenneth. *Minnesota in the Civil War: An Illustrated History*. St. Paul: Minnesota Historical Society Press, 2000.

Dunn, James Taylor. *St. Croix: Midwest Border River*. St. Paul: Minnesota Historical Society Press, 1979.

Easton, Augustus. *History of the St. Croix Valley*. Chicago: H. C. Cooper Jr. and Co., 1909.

Engquist, Anna and Willard Rosenfelt, eds. *Washington: A History of the Minnesota County*. Stillwater, MN: Washington County Historical Society, 1997.

Folsom, W. H. C. *Fifty Years in the Northwest*. 1888. Reprint: Taylors Falls, MN: Taylors Falls Historical Society, 1999.

Folwell, William Watts. *History of Minnesota*. 4 vols. St. Paul: Minnesota Historical Society Press, 1925.

Fowler, Orson S. *The Octagon House: A Home for All, or A New, Cheap, Convenient, and Superior Mode of Building*. 1848. Reprint: New York: Dover Publications, 1973.

Goodman, Robert. *History of Washington County: Gateway to Minnesota History*. Stillwater, MN: Washington County Historical Society, 2008.

Hackl, Lloyd et al. *History of Chisago County, 1851–2001*. Lindström, MN: Chisago County Historical Society, 2001.

Holmquist, June Drenning, ed. *They Chose Minnesota: A Survey of the State's Ethnic Groups.* St. Paul: Minnesota Historical Society Press, 1981.

Johnston, Patricia Condon. *Stillwater: Minnesota's Birthplace.* 1982. Reprint: Afton, MN: Afton Historical Society Press, 1995.

McMahon, Eileen and Theodore Karamanski. *Time and the River: A History of the St. Croix: A Historic Resource Study of the St. Croix National Scenic Riverway.* Omaha, NE: National Park Service, U.S. Department of the Interior, 2002.

Neill, Rev. Edward D. *History of Washington County and the St. Croix Valley including the Explorers and Pioneers of Minnesota.* Minneapolis: Northstar Publishing Company, 1881.

Norelius, Theodore A. *Pioneer Traces In and Near Chisago Lakes Area.* Privately published, 1971.

Pratt, George B. *The Valley of the St. Croix. Picturesque and Descriptive.* Neenah, WI: Art Publishing Company, 1888. Reprint with introduction by James Taylor Dunn, Stillwater MN: Croixside Press, 1970.

Robb, Edwin G. *Afton Remembered.* Afton, MN: Afton Historical Society Press, 1996.

Roney, E. L. *Looking Backward: A Compilation of More Than a Century of St. Croix Valley History.* Stillwater, MN: Stillwater Gazette, 1970.

Singley, Grover. "Retracing the Military Road from Point Douglas to Superior." *Minnesota History* (Spring 1967): 233–47.

Thilgen, Dean. *Valley Rails: A History of Railroads in the St. Croix Valley.* Stillwater, MN: Privately published, 1990.

Waters, Thomas F. *Streams and Rivers of Minnesota.* Minneapolis: University of Minnesota Press, 1977.

WPA Guide to Minnesota. Compiled and written by the Federal Writers' Project of the Works Progress Administration. 1938. Reprint: St. Paul: Minnesota Historical Society Press, 1985.

WPA Guide to Wisconsin. Compiled and written by the Federal Writers' Project of the Works Progress Administration. 1941. Reprint: St. Paul: Minnesota Historical Society Press, 2006.

INDEX

Page numbers in *italics* refer to illustrations; those followed by *m* refer to maps.